COMING OF AGE

Overcoming Trauma to Achieve Self-Determination

Elaine Alec

Coming of Age
Copyright © 2025 by Elaine Alec

All rights reserved. No part of this publication may be reproduced, distributed, or transmitted in any form or by any means, including photocopying, recording, or other electronic or mechanical methods, without the prior written permission of the author, except in the case of brief quotations embodied in critical reviews and certain other non-commercial uses permitted by copyright law.

Tellwell Talent
www.tellwell.ca

ISBN
978-1-77962-919-7 (Paperback)
978-1-77962-920-3 (eBook)

TABLE OF CONTENTS

An Invitation to Courage v
On Capitalization ix
Introduction xi

Chapter 1	The People of the Stories 1
Chapter 2	Storyteller 10
Chapter 3	How Do We Decolonize? 22
Chapter 4	Identity 34
Chapter 5	The Four Siblings 44
Chapter 6	Buckskin Ties 58
Chapter 7	Modern Mentorship 74
Chapter 8	Four Food Chiefs 88
Chapter 9	Spirit Helper 95
Chapter 10	Little Sibling and Patience 114
Chapter 11	People-Eaters 124
Chapter 12	No One Listens These Days 128
Chapter 13	Freedom 131
Chapter 14	The Courage to be Ourselves 136
Chapter 15	The Ultimate Coyote Teaching 140
Chapter 16	Standing by Water 146
Chapter 17	Coming Home 160

Acknowledgements 167
About the Author 175

AN INVITATION TO COURAGE

A Reflection from Jennifer Pastiloff

I knew from the moment I heard Jennifer Pastiloff speak in Miami in April 2022 that I wanted to connect with her. There was something in the way she spoke about being human that stayed with me long after I left the room.

As I neared the final edits of *Coming of Age*, I knew she was the one I wanted to ask to write a reflection. But it took me months to ask. I kept hearing her own words—her reminders to just *do the thing*.

When I finally reached out, it wasn't just admiration. It was because I believe our work is connected. As I listened to her speak, I recognized something familiar—the way she held space, invited people into their own truths, and taught not from a pedestal, but from deep inside the human experience. It was decolonizing. It was Indigenous knowledge in action. It was ancestral wisdom moving through her, whether she named it that way or not.

And that is the heart of this book—reclaiming what has always been ours. Decolonizing is not just about systems or policies; it is about being human. It is about stepping out of shame, out of silence, and into the fullness of ourselves.

Jennifer's book, *On Being Human*, cracked something open in me. It called me to be braver, to step deeper into who I say I am. And that is exactly what *Coming of Age* asks of you, too.

Jennifer didn't write this reflection to explain me or my work. She wrote it because she felt something in these pages that called to her own journey. I invite you to sit with her words before stepping into this book. Let them remind you that this work—this remembering—is for all of us.

—*Elaine Alec*

A Reflection from Jennifer Pastiloff

There's something I say to myself every day upon waking as a prayer, an invocation, an invitation, a ritual. Even before I take my first sip of coffee, I whisper, *May I have the courage to be who I say I am.*

I use whatever works, something I refer to as *The School Of Whatever Works* (barring you're not intentionally hurting yourself or others), in order to help me stay in alignment with who I say I am. Before you correct me—as people have attempted to do when they feel my sentence is somehow misworded—I must clarify that I intentionally put the word *say* in there.

May I have the courage to be who I say I am.

Because fact is, we do get to say who we are. Despite a contrary belief we may have been indoctrinated with, we get to define ourselves for ourselves. We get to decide who we want to be and how we want to live our lives, rather than letting others do so.

Within the pages of *Coming of Age*, the beautiful book you now hold in your hands, Elaine Alec reminds us that the journey of identity is not simply about knowing who you are—it's about cultivating the courage to live in alignment with that knowledge. I knew when I read the first paragraph of this book why I was called to write this reflection. But when I got to those particular lines, I understood even more deeply.

When we have the courage to live in alignment with who we want to be, our calling—as well as our people—show up with utter clarity. Books land in our laps that we feel divinely connected to, love shows up in forms we never could have imagined, stories find us that we would have never heard otherwise. Synchronicity sprouts everywhere, and the thing is, we are actually able to recognize it.

This might feel like some sort of magic trick. In a way, it is—but not the kind where you're manipulated into believing something that isn't really there. This is the truest magic there is. The kind that emerges when you refuse to allow your identity to be stripped away any longer. When you reclaim parts of yourself that were hidden—whether by you, or intentionally hidden by others—you also reclaim your roots, your heritage, your *youness*. And once you have that, anything is possible.

Elaine shows us this with her bravery, resilience, storytelling, refusal to hide in shame, and her fierce commitment to decolonizing.

I felt a shame rising in me at how little I knew about Indigenous Peoples and their actual histories as I read this book. The brutality they suffered, how much was stolen from them, how much has been lost. Sure, I knew some. But the extent to which I allowed myself to *not* know was astounding.

Instead of spiraling in shame, though, I put into practice something I call *Shame Loss*, whereupon you refuse to hide in shame. I realized that so much of what Elaine writes is about this very refusal. It's what she is doing in publishing *Coming of Age*. So, instead of letting shame swallow me, I kept reading and learning and doubling down on my commitment to be of service. To be what I call an *I got you* person.

She writes about how *now* is the time for her to tell the stories of her people. Being an *I got you* person means helping to carry the threads of those stories so they can cast a wider net—so that no more than what has already been lost disappears.

It takes a village, they say. I don't know who *they* are, but it's true. Elaine's elders knew that it took a village, and they were the actual village. They were all part of something that together made up the whole.

When you read this book, you too will see how much of that way of living has fallen away. It's up to us to get it back. We can, if we have the courage to be who we say we are.

—*Jennifer Pastiloff,* author of *On Being Human: A Memoir of Waking Up, Living Real, and Listening Hard*, recognized by *People Magazine* as one of the best new books upon its release, and the forthcoming *Proof of Life: Let Go, Let Love, and Stop Looking for Permission to Live Your Life*, scheduled for release on July 8, 2025.

ON CAPITALIZATION

This book's approach to capitalization is inspired by the practice of modern syilx storytellers who use writing to share our teachings, a practice I first observed in an IndigiNews article by syilx journalist kelsie kilawna. Syilx people are considered egalitarian, which means we honour the belief that no one being or thing is inherently above another. By refraining from capitalizing certain words, I am respecting a worldview in which all life holds equal value—not just humans, but all beings.

I have chosen to capitalize the terms **Indigenous Peoples** and **Animal People**. I do so not to place them above others, but to honour their significance in our culture and teachings. The term **Indigenous Peoples** is capitalized in recognition of the hard work done by Indigenous advocates at the United Nations, which established us as distinct groups with unique rights and identities, worthy of international recognition and respect. Similarly, **Animal People** is capitalized because they are honoured as important figures in our written stories—teachers, guides, and relatives who were within our world before humans.

Throughout this book, I refrain from using capitalization to signal importance in most cases, as our syilx values are inherently egalitarian. Every being—human, plant, animal, or land—holds an equal right to life. This is why I do not capitalize words related to my people, our stories, or our communities. This approach reflects our understanding that no being stands above another. We are all part of the interconnected web of life.

I hope this approach allows you to experience these stories through a syilx lens, in a way that respects our teachings of humility and interconnectedness.

INTRODUCTION

Colonialism is killing Indigenous Peoples. It has woven itself so deeply into our systems, our lands, and our lives that its impacts reach beyond our communities, affecting the entire human family. Its weight bears down on Indigenous men, women, children, and elders, stripping us of our connection to who we are meant to be.

For Indigenous men colonialism is relentless, reinforcing the belief that they must be hard, emotionless, and unyielding, qualities that sever them from their true selves. Each time I look at my oldest son, Kyle, I see the hopes of our ancestors coming true, defying colonial expectations. His gentleness, strength, and open-heartedness are reminders of what our people are capable of when we hold onto our truth. He stands as a symbol of resilience against the forces that try to shape him into something he is not.

But the impact of colonialism is not limited to Indigenous men or even to Indigenous Peoples. The structures that dehumanize and oppress us are the same ones that perpetuate disconnection, loneliness, and suffering across all of humanity. Colonialism fosters a world where power, control, and division are upheld at the expense of love, unity, and compassion. It teaches all people—not just Indigenous Peoples—to be suspicious of their emotions, to fear vulnerability, and to value individualism over community. This unrelenting push for domination and suppression does more than harm us. It stifles our humanness everywhere.

When I travelled through the province of British Columbia in 2019, I heard one message repeated that has stayed with me ever since: "The answer to trauma and violence in our communities is coming-of-age." At the time I didn't fully understand what this meant, but I have come to see that the tradition we call "coming-of-age" is about cultivating safe spaces. It is an understanding that, as human beings, we will inevitably experience pain and hardship. This is a fact of life, and yet colonialism has taught us to avoid our feelings, leaving us unable to process or regulate ourselves through difficult times.

Coming-of-age is the work of reconnecting with ourselves and each other. It is about remembering who we are and embracing the emotional and spiritual growth that we must go through to overcome trauma. This book is a combination of teachings that I hope will open an understanding that we, as humans, are *all* entitled to this work—that coming-of-age is for everyone and that it holds the power to heal.

By the time I turned forty-three years old, I had lost three men who had grown up with me: Kenny Phillip, Davis George, and David Dennis Jr. All three had seen me at my worst, never judged me, and always encouraged me to get my act together. They saw something in me that I didn't, and it was the loss of these men that made me realize the true extent of colonialism's impact—not just on individual lives but on entire communities.

Losing them made me more committed than ever to speak out, speak up, and speak loud, to carry the strength they saw in me, and to honour their belief in my potential. This book is dedicated to them. Their spirits are a testament to the beauty and potential that colonialism seeks to erase but can never fully extinguish.

When I got sober they were still struggling with alcoholism and addictions, yet they never tried to hold me back, nor did they resent my journey. Unlike other friends who teased me, these men simply loved me as I was. In my journey to healing I hope I gave them a glimpse of what was possible—that maybe one day they too could find peace and freedom from the burdens colonialism placed on them.

My son Kyle's journey gives me hope, not only for Indigenous men but for all people. He shows that we can cultivate a path rooted in love, connection, and community rather than domination, separation, and fear.

Colonialism hasn't just hurt Indigenous Peoples, its poison has seeped into all parts of society, isolating us from each other. We are all tied together, and when one of us is hurt it ripples out and affects everyone. Our healing isn't ours alone to carry; it's something we're meant to do together. As we fight for Indigenous resilience, for safe spaces to reclaim our stories and our strength, we are cultivating a world where everyone, Indigenous and non-Indigenous, can live in harmony.

Coming-of-Age is my commitment to those three men I lost, to my children, and to all those who carry the scars of colonialism. It is a testament to the strength of our people, our families, and our communities, a strength that endures despite centuries of attempted erasure. I hope this journey opens hearts and minds to the power of coming-of-age as a pathway to healing and self-determination.

The healing we're seeking can't be done alone. It's a collective journey, a remembering of who we're meant to be as people connected to each other, to the land, and to something bigger than ourselves. I believe this work can help accelerate the human collective's understanding that we can live and think different by remembering who we are.

When we remember who we are and recognize that we belong, we begin to break down the walls colonialism built between us. We begin to see that we belong to each other, to our families, to our communities, and to our lands. Our healing is meant to be shared.

Kenny Phillip

Kenny was a lifelong friend who carried a lot of struggles and pain, working through it all his life. Both of us were angry about so many things, but we also saw a light in each other. Growing up on the Penticton Indian Band reserve, we spent our teenage years doing stupid things, yet there were moments when we'd find ourselves alone, talking for hours about the state of the world and our community.

Those conversations grounded me. Kenny had a way of challenging me to think bigger, to believe that we could make a difference. He was brilliant, with endless ideas about what our lives could be and how we might make things better. We'd argue and challenge each other, sometimes getting mad over our different views, but underneath it all we saw something in each other. Even back then we knew we were supposed to be doing more to be better. Kenny's friendship was a lifeline for me. He believed in me when I didn't believe in myself, and he made me feel like I wasn't alone in the world.

We wove in and out of each other's lives. Sometimes he'd show up with that familiar excitement, eager to tell me about all the good things he was doing, celebrating his time sober and sharing his dreams for the future. And in the times he struggled, he didn't hide his reality from me. He was open about his hardships, and he trusted me enough to share the weight he was carrying.

There was a time in my thirties when I was experiencing PTSD and couldn't function. I had been sexually assaulted and was spiralling, lost in fear and uncertainty about how I would make it through. Kenny found me in that dark space. He came up to me, wrapped me in a long hug, and told me he had my back. In that moment his presence and those words gave me the strength and courage to keep going. I knew the darkness he was carrying, the struggles he fought inside himself, and the fact that he took the time to comfort me meant more than he ever knew. He made me feel like I didn't have to carry it all alone.

He passed away on his birthday in 2018. His life was a cycle of struggle, moving in and out of sobriety, but every time I saw him he'd still encourage me. Losing him stirred up feelings I wasn't ready to face. I didn't know how to process the reality that I was going to start losing friends who were fighting the same battles with alcohol and addiction.

So much of Kenny's pain was rooted in intergenerational trauma. His parents had been part of the Sixties Scoop, taken from their family and culture and forced to grow up in a system that aimed to erase who they were. That trauma bled into Kenny's life, shaping how he saw himself and the world around him. From a young age he was judged, harassed, and labelled as trouble. Colonial stereotypes were shadows that followed him, constant reminders that society saw him as less than. He was told time and time again that he didn't belong, that he wasn't worthy of a good life. Colonialism made him feel that all he deserved was struggle.

But he wasn't alone in his fight. His parents worked tirelessly to help him heal, to break the cycle of pain that had been passed down. His friends and family surrounded him with love, showing him over and over how cherished he was and trying to help him see himself through their eyes. We all wanted him to feel the love wrapped around him, so he would know he was worthy of a good life. But addiction is cunning, baffling, and powerful. It grips onto pain and twists it, making it hard to see a way out. Even with all the love in the world, sometimes the weight of trauma and addiction becomes a cage.

Still, when Kenny's light was able to break through, it shone so brightly. He took pride in his sober days, celebrating them with a smile that reached his eyes. He'd share his dreams with a spark, full of ideas and hopes for a better life—not just for himself but for everyone he loved. He wanted so much more, and he deserved it all. But colonialism's hold runs deep, and it takes more than individual strength and love to break free from trauma that's been woven into us for generations.

Kenny fought hard, harder than anyone should have to. But he was up against forces that have crushed so many of our people, and sometimes even the brightest light can get lost in that darkness. His life showed me the depths of intergenerational trauma, the way it weaves through our lives and shapes how we see ourselves and what we believe we deserve. Losing him reminded me how vital our shared healing is, how important it is to reclaim the parts of ourselves that colonialism tried to erase. And it made me even more determined to work toward a world where our people know they are loved and worthy, and that they belong.

Davis George

In 2020, Davis—Kyle's dad—told me he had too many health issues to name. He was the kind of guy who would brush everything off, cracking jokes to lighten the mood when he sensed the worry in my voice. No matter how many times he injured himself or got sick, he refused to go to the hospital. It wasn't just pride—he didn't trust the doctors. He'd been treated poorly too many times, and he felt the hospital made him worse instead of better.

The racism he experienced in the healthcare system, the lack of meaningful support, the way they assumed he was just another Indigenous man wasting their time—all of it pushed him farther away from the help he needed. This is one of the ways colonialism is killing us. It's not just about the past, it's in the systems that are supposed to care for us but instead tell us over and over that our lives aren't worth much.

Davis was gifted in so many ways. He was one of the hardest workers I've known, and he carried himself with respect. Back when we were teenagers he'd work long days in his dad's hay and potato fields, putting in twelve hours, then head off to his apprenticeship at a mechanic's shop. Later he put in even more long days working maintenance at the airport in Penticton, British Columbia. Eventually he took on a role as a mechanic and maintenance supervisor for our community, the Penticton Indian Band. He was always cruising around the rez, waving at everyone or stopping by just to visit and crack a joke.

My mom, Sophie, loved Davis. We had some boxing gloves at the house, and one day we were fooling around, sparring for fun. Davis was a big guy, six-two, and he was going easy on me and my sister but still managing to beat us effortlessly. Then my mom, all five foot two of her, decided she wasn't going to just stand by. She grabbed a pair of gloves and told him to bring it on. He couldn't believe it. He started laughing and tapping out gently, playing along.

At one point they messed up their timing. Just as he was releasing a tap, my mom stepped forward and he caught her right in the forehead. She staggered back, and for a split second I saw shock and horror on his face. But she started laughing, and we all joined in. I'll never forget the look on his face: half terrified, half amused. Moments like that made their connection special. He adored her and brought out her playful side, teasing her in a way that made her feel young again.

But Davis was more than just a hard worker and jokester. He was an artist too, a carver and metalworker, and he put his heart into every creation. He carved a ceremonial pipe and a bone-handled knife for my mom. These weren't just objects to him, they were gifts that came from a place of respect and love. We put an artist portfolio together so he could apply to the Emily Carr University of Art + Design in Vancouver. He got serious about school, doing what he needed to get the credits, and I helped him with his English assignments (okay, I did his English assignments for him). We thought it was ridiculous that he had to pass English to become an artist. But in the end he just couldn't leave home. To him, home had everything he needed.

Davis had a light about him, but like so many young Indigenous men he was constantly reminded that he wasn't worth anything. Society, teachers, and even some people in our community judged him harshly, partially because his dad was white and had a complicated history in our community. Davis struggled with abuse as a child, and he was an altar boy at the Catholic church on our reserve. He was never silent about how much it had harmed him.

He started drinking young, and like so many of us he got into trouble—stealing, speeding, breaking and entering. If there's one thing I know about drinking and dealing with judgment from your own community, it eventually gets you to a place where you don't care anymore. You keep going until you start to believe every harsh word they throw at you. Slowly his light began to dim, and the only thing that kept it burning at all were his kids.

In the last few months of his life, though, something shifted. He began to brighten again. He'd call me with new ideas, talking about renewable energy and ways to start a business so he wouldn't have to rely on hard labour. After all the years of wearing down his body, both from the work and from drinking, his health was failing.

When he finally saw how sick he was, he made the decision to get sober. It was like his mind had come alive again—he couldn't stop thinking, dreaming. For the first time in a long time he started to believe in himself again.

He was so proud of my writing. When I sent him an electronic copy of my book, he told me firmly that he would like a paperback copy he could hold. Back when we were kids he was the one person I shared my poems and stories with, and he would always tell me I'd be a writer one day. In his last months he kept reminding me to slow down, to not work so hard. Whenever he saw my car at my family's house in Penticton, he'd stop by just to say hi. I'd do the same at his place. Occasionally he'd call me after a hospital visit, his voice filled with that old spark, his mind brimming with ideas.

I think in those final months he started to see just how fragile life really is. He found the courage to start dreaming again.

Colonialism tried to take that courage from him, to make him believe he wasn't worth a better life. That's what colonialism does, tries to keep our people disconnected and numb, questioning our own value. That's why coming-of-age is so important.

Coming-of-age is about reclaiming who we are, our worth, and our connection to each other and our culture. It's the work of breaking down colonial walls, teaching ourselves and our children that they belong, they are loved, and they deserve a life full of meaning and connection.

I think of Davis when it snows. That was our playtime. I was always the serious one—I thought being silly was immature. But Davis brought the kid out of me. He taught me how to play and have fun, how to drive fast and drift around corners, how to ride a dirt bike and ski. He even tried, with no success, to teach me how to snowboard. Every winter when the snow starts to fall I feel that same inspiration to write, and I know he's proud of me for doing what I always said I was going to do.

David Dennis Jr.

David was from the nuu-chah-nulth nation. I met him when I was eighteen, living with my mom on the Penticton Indian Band reserve. He was recruiting for the Native Youth Movement, which he'd co-founded alongside the Westcoast Warriors Society. Together they travelled from Burnt Church, New Brunswick, to some of the most remote communities in British Columbia, blocking highways and shutting down government offices to fight for our rights and demand justice from the government and corporations that were continually oppressing Indigenous Peoples. David saw me on the news once—I'd organized a school walkout to support the Gustafsen Lake standoff in 1995—and from then on we were connected.

We were part of something bigger, something our fathers had fought for too. We were "AIM Kids," children of the American Indian Movement, raised with the fire of resistance in our bones. AIM wasn't just a group, it was a way of life. Founded in 1968, it was created to stand up against the systemic poverty, police brutality, and discrimination that Indigenous people were facing every day. Our fathers fought to bring back dignity and justice, and that's what David carried forward. Growing up as AIM Kids, we were taught to stand up, carry our warrior blood with pride, and always remember where we came from. David held on to that, even as life tried to wear him down.

In 2019, David reached out to me. He'd been diagnosed with liver cancer and was committed to staying sober. Even while facing his own mortality he wanted to talk about sobriety, about life, and, as always, he wanted to share his ideas. He was in pain, yet he was still thinking about our people. We talked about the healthcare system—the same system that's supposed to help us but instead is steeped in racism. He talked about how Indigenous people are treated like they don't matter. Colonialism isn't just something in our history books, it's alive and kicking in every part of the healthcare system, telling us we're less than, that we're not worth saving. For David, going to the hospital felt like a gamble, and when he was diagnosed with liver disease the healthcare system showed its true colours with its abstinence policy.

This policy says that people with alcohol-use disorder have to abstain from drinking for six months before they're even considered for a liver transplant. David was completely shut out. It didn't matter that he was sober and fighting for his life. The policy wasn't there to help, it was there to judge, to shut the door on Indigenous people struggling with alcohol.

In 2015, the Truth and Reconciliation Commission of Canada called for systemic changes in healthcare. But here we are, still facing policies that deny Indigenous people a fighting chance. David wasn't going to take it lying down. Alongside the Union of BC Indian Chiefs and the Frank Paul Society,[1] he filed a human rights complaint to challenge the abstinence policy, knowing full well that this fight wasn't just about him. "If I don't make it, I want the UBCIC and Frank Paul Society to carry on and get rid of this lethal form of racism," he said. He was thinking of every Indigenous person facing the same barriers, being told their life wasn't worth saving.

In our last conversations he shared his dreams with me. He wanted the taxes from alcohol sales to fund long-term recovery centres and give people a basic income while they focused on healing. "How can anyone recover if they're just trying to survive?" he asked me. He saw things with a clarity that only comes when you know your time is limited, and he was still dreaming of a better world for our people.

We met in Vancouver that December. He joked about how easy the younger generation has it. "Can you believe how spoiled these youth are nowadays?" he laughed. "They get their travel covered, they get a seat at the table. Back in our day we had to hitchhike, crash wherever we could, and force our ways into the chiefs' meetings just to be heard." But he was proud that he'd fought to create space for our youth.

He asked me about the work I was doing, and I shared how his ideas lined up with what I was doing through the Path Forward Women & Girls Community Safety Sessions. I'd been travelling across BC, holding circles to talk about violence against Indigenous women, girls, and our 2SLGBTQQIA+ relatives to help create an action plan for our province. People shared about the need for healing centres, places that would make them feel

---

[1] The Frank Paul Society is a Vancouver-based organization established to address police accountability and the treatment of Indigenous Peoples in the criminal justice system. David served as its first president.

safe. But they also talked about something deeper: the need to bring back our coming-of-age ceremonies, the practices that root us in who we are.

I told David about this and he nodded, understanding exactly what I meant. "We need to do coming-of-age with our babies and children again," I said. He replied, "We also need to do it with us—the adults who never got it." I pulled out my phone and made a note of it, because I knew his words would guide me. David understood that self-determination isn't just about policies or rights, it's about healing from within. It's about going back to our teachings, grounding ourselves in the parts of our culture that colonialism tried to erase.

When we talk about self-determination, it's often about getting a voice in government or a seat at the table. But David and I knew that real self-determination means something much deeper. It means reclaiming who we are on our own terms, breaking free from the limitations colonial systems try to place on us. Self-determination is about building a world that lifts us up, that honours our strengths, our histories, our ways of being.

Coming-of-age is part of that. It's more than a ceremony, it's a way of telling our youth that they are worthy, they belong. It's about showing them that they're connected—to their families, to their land, to each other. And it's for us, too, for the generations who missed out on that grounding who are still piecing ourselves back together.

Self-determination starts with knowing ourselves, connecting to our roots, our histories, and building a future that honours those things. In every circle I sat in, every call for healing, every plea to bring back our coming-of-age ceremonies, I felt the power of our people reclaiming their right to be whole.

Colonialism tried to take that from us, to sever us from our ways and tell us we were less. But through this work we are showing that those ways are still alive in us, that they are stronger than anything colonialism can throw at us. Self-determination is a journey back to ourselves, to our communities, to each other. It's about looking within, remembering who we are and teaching our children to do the same.

Self-determination is more than a word we use to assert our rights and jurisdiction in political and governing spaces. It is a process and a pathway to healing for each one of us. How do we do that? Where does it begin?

It starts by going to the water and looking within.

Chapter 1

THE PEOPLE OF THE STORIES

As soon as the snow begins to fall I feel a pull deep within me to write and share stories. There's something about winter that brings the stories to life, like they're drifting down with the snow, ready to be woven into words. It is December and I'm sitting in my living room in secwepemculuwx, also known as Shuswap territory, in tk'emlúps te secwépemc (Kamloops, British Columbia). This is my father's, Saul Kenzie Basil's, territory, and these lands have their own voice. It feels familiar yet slightly distant, like a memory I am still getting to know.

As I watch the snow fall now, I hear a voice in my mind. It's a gentle hum, a lulling tone that rises and falls and sounds like home to me. It's the sound of elders, their voices rich with wisdom, sharing stories and teachings carried on the winter air. They are speaking nsyilxcen, the language I grew up to. This is the time of year when our ancestors shared their knowledge, in the quiet months when the land rests and we gather close. I can feel their presence, hear their words as if they are right beside me, speaking from a place beyond time and inviting me to listen, to remember, to share.

I moved to Kamloops when I was 38, but now, at 47, I've found myself back in Penticton, BC, on my mother's homeland, syilx territory. I came back for my daughter, Phoenix, who is going through her coming-of-age. This is a time when she needs to feel a deep sense of belonging and connection to who she is. I couldn't finish this book until I did the work I needed to do with her, to take what I've learned and share it with her.

Over the last few years I watched my daughter lose herself. She had been drawn into a culture of dance—ballet, jazz, tap, musical theatre, and acro—which, despite its beauty, is a deeply colonial institution. She drifted farther and farther from her true self, absorbing their messages of perfectionism and shame until her spirit and light began to dim. She started to believe those lies, to think that her worth was something to be measured, controlled, and polished to someone else's standard.

So we made the decision to come home. And the moment we returned to syilx territory, something shifted. I watched her start to call her spirit back, reconnecting with our family, our community, our nation, and the land. Here she can finally feel that she is part of something bigger, something real and alive. She can see that she belongs, not to anyone's standards but her own, to this land, this family, this way of life. It's a journey we're taking together, and it's healing us both in ways I didn't expect.

My daughter was named after my mom, Sophie. Not her English name, but her nsyilxcen one. My grandma didn't give my mom a name on the day she was born. She went without it for many years. My mom struggled with alcoholism for a long time, and it wasn't until she got sober that my grandma finally gave her a name. She named her maxaknitkw, which means White Grizzly Bear Woman. My mom was excited, proud of this name, until another elder told her she didn't deserve it. They said it was too big, that maxaknitkw was the name of a hereditary chief who spoke to the water people, a name powerful and important. I remember my mom sharing that experience with me, how heartbroken she was.

When my daughter was born my mom passed her name to her. She named Phoenix maxaknitkw. In our teachings we're told that when you're given a name you carry the strength and wisdom of all the ancestors who held it before you, and that you will add your own spirit to it, shaping it for the generations to come. I will spend every day of my life teaching Phoenix that her name is not too big for her. I want her to know she is worthy of every part of it, that she belongs to this lineage and has everything within her that she needs to honour it.

Phoenix carries herself in a way that reminds me of the strength in her name. I tease her sometimes, because she is timid and scared of so many things. She struggles with anxiety and the way the world works. She is aware of everything around her and how people's actions impact the world. She has an intense sensitivity to justice and always speaks up, even when she gets bullied for it. She's constantly being told she's making a big deal about nothing, but it's because she sees what others don't. She is courageous, showing me what it means to feel the fear and do it anyway. She's adding to the spirit of maxaknitkw in her own way, teaching me that strength doesn't mean the absence of fear, it means moving forward with it, grounded in who you are. I am so grateful to watch her carry this name forward, knowing she is shaping it with every step.

When Phoenix was just six years old she starred in *Holy Angels*, a short documentary that brings to life the story of Lena Wandering Spirit, an Indigenous woman who attended the Holy Angels Residential School in 1963. Watching Phoenix dance through the empty halls of an abandoned building, embodying Lena's memories, was a powerful reminder of our resilience. Her movements in that space felt like a reclamation, breathing life into a place marked by pain and honouring the strength of all who endured.

Directed by Jay Cardinal Villeneuve, *Holy Angels* captures Canada's colonial past through a child's eyes, with Phoenix's portrayal of Lena reminding us of the healing journey so many of us continue. This film was recognized with accolades like the Founder's Award at the 2018 Yorkton Film Festival, and it featured at the 2017 ImagineNATIVE Film and Media Arts Festival.

Phoenix used her ballet skills and her gifts in jingle-dress dancing to share the story in a beautiful way. I have never seen such determination in someone so young. The producers told me that Phoenix had all the skills to do this for a career, and that she was the most dedicated and patient child actor they had ever worked with, including ones twice her age.

My Uncle Steve Basil told me, "That light in Phoenix's eyes is the light that all our children carried before they went to residential school. That is the light we want all our children to have again." Ever since then I have worked hard to make sure no one dims her light by reminding her who she is and where she comes from. I help her through moments when others try to tell her she is wrong for speaking up. I teach her to feel all the pain but know she will move through it, survive, and come out stronger.

It hasn't been easy. Social media, online gaming, racism, and children raised in unsafe spaces have challenged her spirit and mental health. Sometimes it's been frightening to see how deeply she feels and how much it affects her. When things got tough I stopped and asked myself how to support her, reminded myself to not make it about me, and to prioritize the cultivation of belonging, connection, and safety for her. I brought her home to my mom's territory, where her belly button is buried. My mom told me that you have to bury a baby's belly button in the land so the child will always know they belong. It will let them know where they come from and where home is, so they will always have a place to return to. The moment my daughter and I came home, something shifted inside of us.

I know that not everyone is tied to these lands in the same way we are, but each of us carries our ancestors within us. We all come from somewhere, from people who had their own lands, their own ways of life, their own understandings of belonging. Even in today's world we can still connect to who we are and where we come from. It's in these connections that we find our true foundation, something deeper and older than the colonial systems around us. This is why so many of us feel lost and struggle within the lives imposed on us: there's a part of us that remembers, that knows this isn't the way we were meant to live. We feel the disconnect, a fracture that needs healing.

But when we remember where we come from and who we are, we begin to feel whole again. And this wholeness doesn't just serve us individually, it ripples outward, impacting how we live together in this place and time. When each of us has a sense of belonging, a connection to something greater, it changes the way we walk on these lands. We learn to walk with respect and care, knowing we are all interconnected. When we each know who we are, when we feel grounded in something beyond ourselves, we create a way of being that honours this land and everyone who lives upon it. This is how we begin to live together in a good way.

I grew up on the Penticton Indian Band reserve, nestled in the Okanagan Valley of southern BC. This is syilx territory, the land of my mother's people. We are also called *okanagan*, but growing up we had our own words for who we are: *sqilx^w* and *suqnaqinx*. Sqilx^w translates to "dream in a spiral." It speaks to the way we see the world, the way we move through it, and the way we are always connected, looping back to our beginnings. Suqnaqinx means "the ones who stand on a mountain and are seen and heard from far away." The anglicized name, "Okanagan," doesn't carry the same depth or power, but we use it to connect with those who might not know our language, to share a piece of who we are.

Our language, nsyilxcen, is more than words, it's a way of understanding the world. It holds our responsibilities, our connection to all living things. In nsyilxcen, we learn that syilx people have a duty to collect and weave together understandings of the world and to intertwine ourselves within the *tmix^w*—the land, the water, the animals, all living things—and its regenerative capacity. This language holds our responsibilities to the land and each other, reminding us that we are part of something much bigger, something that is constantly renewing and sustaining itself.

We are known as the "people of the stories," and our stories are more than tales, they are guides carrying the teachings of how to live in a good way. Our people are also known as the "people with the power to dream." These translations into English feel limited, but they're the closest we have to explain the depths of who we are. The people from my mother's territory are *sn'klip*'s—Coyote's—people, and with that comes the responsibility to teach. We were given the duty long ago to share our knowledge with the world, to ensure that others learn to live in harmony with all beings.

As we were growing up, the elders in our community shared their knowledge freely, openly, with a generosity that was rooted in the understanding that knowledge isn't meant to be hoarded. They'd tell us, "Knowledge is no good if you're not sharing it." They knew that their wisdom held a balance, a reciprocity, that extended beyond the human world to include all living things. We were taught that knowledge has the power to guide, to heal, to help others live in a good way, and that "you don't know what you don't know." This humility is a cornerstone of our teachings—it reminds us to keep learning, to keep listening, and to understand that there is always more to know.

And so, as I sit here back in my mother's territory, feeling the snow coming down the mountains, I feel that responsibility rising within me. The stories want to be told, the teachings want to be shared. The voices of my ancestors are close, reminding me that I am just one part of a larger whole. This is what it means to be syilx, to be okanagan, to be sqilx^w. It's a way of being that reaches back through generations, a way of knowing that ties us to the land, to each other, and to all things. As I write I am honouring that connection, weaving myself into the story, becoming part of the dream that spirals back to the beginning and forward to all that is yet to come.

Wintertime is sacred for storytelling. It's when our people slow down, rest, plan, and pray for the next seasons. We share these stories in the lodge and pit house. The lodge is where we hold a ceremony called the winter dance, some call it a winter hop. It's a place for singing, dancing, and praying for all living beings. It's a time when people share their songs with others, discuss important matters, and prepare for the year to come. Sometimes we share visions or ideas about what we need to do to make sure everyone is cared for.

When my sister and I were little girls, my mom would take us to the winter dance to learn discipline. We didn't know much about the ceremony, we went simply because that's what we were told to do. We would sit and listen to everything being said and pray, and we were not allowed to leave until the singing was done.

The lodge has a door person who only lets people in and out when it's time, usually after the important business has been carried out. We limit the number of times the door is opened because the spirits are strong and moving about.

The pit house is where we live during the winter, taking our time to tell stories in their entirety. Some stories take days to tell. They guide us in doing things in a good way: how we behave, how we carry ourselves, how we interact within our families and nation, and how we care for the land.

We were always guests at these dances our relatives hosted. They carried the instructions, the language, the songs, and the ways. That's how they took care of our people. Every family was given a responsibility to care for the community, the nation, and the land. We all relied on each other to present what we knew, with each family passing down specific responsibilities through generations. Some families carried the knowledge of hunting, some of medicine, some of governance and laws, some of fishing, some of tending different areas of the land. No role was considered more important than the others.

In our villages, everyone has a role. There are those who teach discipline and how to keep the peace. As I share stories from our language and lands, it's important to remember that the English words we use don't hold the same meanings as they do for people who grew up with English as their first language. Discipline, for most people, often implies harshness, something imposed by others. But for me, discipline is something I carry within myself—it's about paying attention, focusing, informing the way I sit and listen. Discipline is something I have to maintain whether someone is watching or not.

Every member of our villages has a responsibility to make sure everyone lives in good health. In the past we understood that for our villages to thrive each of us needed to be well, so we could take care of one another and sustain our way of life. We knew there would be times when we'd all need to work hard and prepare together. For that everyone needed to be healthy, physically, mentally, and emotionally.

As long as you follow the customs and laws within your community, you have a right to be there. But if you choose not to follow the laws, you live by yourself, off the land, away from the community. When I was about ten years old we were driving by a mountain, and my mom told me a story about a couple who had an affair and had to go live on that mountain alone. She said, "A long time ago, when people didn't want to be married to each other anymore, they would tell their families and then they would have to go live on their own for one year. If they survived that time and still wanted to be together, they could rejoin the community."

All our laws exist to remind us of our responsibility to future generations. Our leaders ensure that there is balance between our human needs, the natural laws, and the land. We understand that when we care for the land, we are also taking care of ourselves and those who come after us. This connection to the land gives us a strong sense of purpose and confidence in ourselves and each other.

The ability to regulate ourselves, to live in harmony with others, comes from our coming-of-age practices. They guide us in understanding who we are and how to conduct ourselves. They teach us resilience, patience, and respect, forming the foundation of our self-determination. Coming-of-age is about learning our roles within the community, knowing what is expected of us, and recognizing our responsibilities, not just to ourselves but to each other and to the land. This is where true self-governance begins, not as something given to us by others but as something deeply rooted within us.

I was taught that good governance means carrying the laws inside us. We know how to act without needing someone to enforce rules. We live this way because we follow the natural laws of the land. We were raised with love and patience, developing a deep understanding of who we are. Discipline was instilled in us from the moment we could learn. When you know who you are and where you come from, you have confidence, patience, respect, and the ability to regulate yourself.

True self-governance and self-determination mean we know how to govern ourselves without enforcement. This way of being is not a system imposed from the outside, it is an agreement we hold within, born from our traditions and carried forward through our coming-of-age practices.

As you think about these teachings, ask yourself what stories have shaped you, and how they guide your actions and values. How connected do you feel to where you come from, and in what ways could that connection be deepened? What does self-governance look like in your life, and how do you carry the responsibilities of your community, land, and ancestors within you? Think about how you can weave your own stories and roots into your daily life, honouring where you come from as you move forward.

Chapter 2

STORYTELLER

Our elders tell us it is important that we share our stories in the way they have been passed on to us. This doesn't mean we're bound to repeat them word for word, but it is important to remember their emotion, songs, and sometimes even shocking details to help us recall the teachings. Some of our stories come across as graphic or funny, because when our emotions are evoked the story becomes a part of us, and this comes out in the telling. Our stories share the natural laws of how to behave and treat all living things. Syilx peoples and the lands have been able to thrive and live in harmony for thousands of years because our laws live inside of us. Our stories make this so.

The human mind has a natural memory and an artificial memory. Natural memory exists from birth, but artificial memory needs to be trained and developed. The human mind easily remembers personal, surprising, physical, sexual, humorous, and relatable information. Songs, poems, images, connections, and visualizations all help train our mind to remember.

We share teachings and protocols through songs and drums. Our language invokes imagery in our minds because it is fundamentally descriptive. It takes a long time for us to translate our language into English because it is composed of imagery in our minds. Our elders say that listening to our language is like watching a picture show in your mind. Our stories are connected to each other, with main characters and connective strands, which makes it easier to build new knowledge upon existing knowledge. Visualization techniques are also utilized within our stories, helping us to remember through land markings. We have land markers represented by water, rocks, mountains, and anomalies in the land throughout our territory to tell us a story, which is a teaching connected to a law about how to be. Every time we pass these markings, we remember the stories. These stories help us remember who we are, where we come from, and how to live well.

Our people not only trained themselves to remember our stories, to make these teachings a part of our whole being, but also to function during times of stress, trauma, and hardship. We are able to regulate our minds and bodies to challenging circumstances and information to survive, and to navigate our villages and lands.

Our people understand that we will suffer from the moment we are born, experiencing pain and trauma. We know that these moments will impact our thinking and focus, and our ability to be effective and contribute.

Throughout my life I've suffered from pain, loss, and traumatic experiences, and during these times my community elders would share their wisdom and experiences with me. They would say that this was a sacred time for my spirit, and it was part of life. The only way to get rid of the pain is to go through it, to feel it. I was not to numb it or ignore it, but experience it, because by going through it I would grow. They would tell me, "We need to become strong through our lives by experiencing hardship and challenges. Every time we get through it, we become stronger. The Creator doesn't just pour strong into the top of your head."

Trauma is recognized as a sacred time, a signal that we need to slow down and be guided through practices that help us move through it, not around it. Ceremony, sweat lodge, cold-water baths, fasting, and training are the ways we support our people through their hardest times. These practices are not only traditions, but vital methods that ground us in the present moment, pulling us out of the parts of our minds that dwell in the past. The sounds, the singing, the feeling of hot and cold, even the pain, all anchor us to the here and now, reminding us of our resilience and our ability to be fully present, even in our suffering. In these moments we connect with the discipline, love, belonging, and safety that help us regulate ourselves and heal.

Trauma isn't something we can escape, it is an inevitable part of being human, something we must move through as part of our journey. When we numb it or push it aside, it lingers unprocessed in our bodies and minds, growing in strength until it shapes our lives in ways we may not recognize. Unacknowledged trauma unsettles the spirit, leading us to act in ways that don't reflect who we truly are. Over time untreated trauma can fester, transforming into fear, disconnection, anger, helplessness, and hopelessness, making it impossible to function with creativity, purpose, or joy. This unhealed pain ripples outward, affecting not just individuals but entire communities, undermining the foundations of our societies.

But when we honour trauma as something sacred that needs tending, we reclaim the power to move through it with courage and presence. By facing our trauma we strengthen our connection to ourselves, our community, and the world around us. This is why we engage in ceremony: to feel the grounding power of being fully here, in the present, supported by the wisdom and presence of our ancestors and each other. In doing so we remind ourselves that trauma, while painful, is also a teacher, guiding us toward resilience and a truer understanding of who we are and what it means to heal.

Today we have more scientific understanding of the brain, confirming what our people have instinctively always known. We now know that when the brain is in trauma mode we operate primarily from the brain stem, which is responsible for survival responses. In this state our decisions and actions come from a place of heightened reactivity, often feeling ineffective, cynical, or helpless. This reactivity is driven by elevated cortisol, a stress hormone that prepares us to fight or flee but, when sustained, reinforces fear-based patterns and clouds our perception of reality. To support someone in moving out of this brain-stem-driven state, we must first establish a sense of safety and connection, which engages the limbic brain. When we feel safe and connected, oxytocin—a hormone associated with trust and bonding—can counterbalance cortisol's effects, helping us regulate emotions and reduce anxiety. Only when these foundational needs for safety and connection are met can we access the cortex, the part of the brain responsible for higher-order thinking, allowing us to make clear, purposeful decisions and to contribute our best to the world around us.

This understanding reminds me of how our teachings have always emphasized the importance of beginning early in nurturing safety, connection, and belonging in our children. It is important to begin teaching our babies the moment they are able to learn, through songs and bedtime stories repeated every night. I have beautiful memories of this and remember the feeling of safety and connection with my *tema*—my mom's mom—as she told me stories. During certain parts she would sing a little song and move her fingers in the air above us to mimic the animals' movements.

As I got older the stories evolved, growing into new teachings and laws. I began to hear variations of these stories and songs from other families and different parts of our nation, each one carrying a teaching I hadn't encountered before. Many times people would criticize others for telling the story "wrong," but the oldest elders would remind us that none of it was wrong—that was just the way it was. This taught us that there is more than one way of knowing and seeing the world, and that our teachings were never about a single, rigid "right" way. It meant that we understood stories could shift depending on where and when they were told, and by whom.

Our stories and language are tied to the land, not to paper. Writing things down can make people believe that what's written is the only truth, the absolute way, which is one of the many false ideas we need to unlearn. Our teachings live in the voices and experiences of those who share them, allowing them to breathe, grow, and change as our people do. This fluidity is not a weakness but a strength, a reminder that there is always room for different perspectives, for new wisdom, and for a deeper understanding of who we are in relation to each other and the world around us.

Our stories help us develop our identities and sense of belonging, grounding us in who we are and where we come from. When we have a strong sense of identity and belonging we feel safe and connected, able to function at the highest level of our minds, bodies, and spirits. We can problem-solve, create, and approach life in a positive way. Without that deep sense of belonging we feel unsafe and disconnected, mistrusting the world around us.

Throughout this book I will do my best to share coming-of-age practices and stories that are meant to connect you to a deeper sense of knowing and understanding. My hope is that these teachings will help you cultivate belonging, connection, safety, and a sense of purpose within yourself. In this way you can begin to move from survival mode into a place of resilience and purpose, finding strength in both the ancient wisdom of our people and the newer insights of science, to live and walk in this world with confidence and peace.

Some people are given the gift of storytelling. When I was little I was told to listen very carefully to our storytellers, elders, and medicine people. Even at that young age I was taught the great responsibility I carried simply by hearing these stories. When our people choose to share stories, it is because they are teaching something vital. These stories are not just memories of the past, they are guides meant to help us make good decisions when the time comes. They are prophecies, reminders that our ancestors foresaw the challenges we'd face and made sure the wisdom we would need was woven into our stories, language, and teachings.

Our elders always told us that things would get worse before they got better, that difficult times were coming. But they also said that if we held tight to our teachings we could move through these hardships, and that these teachings weren't just for us but for anyone willing to learn. Our *cepcaptikʷł*, our stories, carry the truths and natural laws that will support anyone who listens with respect. They remind us how to live in balance, how to find strength in our connections to each other, and how to honour and care for all living beings.

Cepcaptikʷł are much more than just tales. They are truths brought to life in the telling, wisdom that survives because it is passed from one person to the next. Learning and teaching cepcaptikʷł is essential because we weren't born with all the answers or a perfect memory of how to live in harmony with the land's laws. We carry memory, but it needs to be cultivated—fed, repeated, and shared. Without these it slips away.

Our teachings guide us to live in respect and reciprocity with all things, carrying instructions that help us move through life's hardest moments with resilience and grace. We have stories about the world before creation, stories of the world's first living beings—the Animal People, sn'klip, and the first humans.

The stories of the world before creation tell of how the Creator brought the world and all its beings into existence. Our stories about the Animal People share teachings about each animal's place and role, guiding us on how to live, how to ensure the regeneration of all life and honour the natural law.

The stories of sn'klip, both a trickster and a hero, teach us about behaviour and choice. Sn'klip does wonderful and terrible things, serving as an example of what we should avoid. Though not perfect and often making mistakes, sn'klip is always given the chance to come back to life, showing us that even when we stray we can return to the path.

Our stories of the first humans are filled with prophecies foretelling what will happen and reminding us of the consequences of our actions. They teach us that when we follow the teachings life will be good, but if we ignore them we will face hardship. Through these stories we understand that our choices shape the world we live in.

I grew up surrounded by elders who only spoke the language. My tema and I would go to community meetings where the elders filled the benches that lined the walls of the community hall, sitting side by side like pillars holding up the room. They would speak through an interpreter, sharing their thoughts and teachings, their voices filling the space with the rhythm and pulse of nsyilxcen. I grew up in a home where my tema only spoke nsyilxcen, and to us it was the language that carried everything we needed to know about who we were and how we should live.

In those days I never thought twice about sharing what we knew or about holding back any part of our teachings. It didn't occur to me that knowledge was something to keep hidden or guarded. For us knowledge isn't something you own or keep to yourself, it's something you give away so it can continue to live and grow in others. I remember hearing a conversation among the elders wherein they spoke about why they didn't like to be called "knowledge keepers." They didn't see themselves as keepers of knowledge, as if knowledge were something to store away. They thought of themselves as guardians who were meant to pass knowledge along, carrying teachings forward so they could be passed on and shared openly.

They believed that knowledge was alive, flowing through people, stories, and songs. Holding on to it would be like trying to stop a river from flowing—it's not meant to be dammed up. It's meant to travel and reach others, especially those who live in our territories, even if they aren't syilx. How are they supposed to know how to act and live respectfully on these lands if they don't know the stories?

The elders understood that if people are to live in harmony with the land, they need to understand its history and teachings.

This knowledge wasn't only for us but for anyone who wanted to live here. Sharing stories wasn't just an act of kindness, it was a responsibility. They believed it was important to offer these teachings freely so that anyone living on this land would know how to walk gently and respectfully. To them, the act of sharing wasn't only about preserving culture, it was about creating a community that could live well together.

So we share our stories with the understanding that they will become a guide for all people here, syilx or not. The teachings in our stories are about how to care for the land, how to respect each other, and how to live in a way that brings balance. Knowledge is meant to be a gift passed on with open hands, shaping everyone who calls this place home.

We have a word in our language, *tmxʷulaxʷ*, one of the first words broken down in English for me. If you asked someone what tmxʷulaxʷ means and they didn't want to dive into its depth or felt pressed for time, they might just say "land." But tmxʷulaxʷ is so much more. It includes everything alive: the land, water, animals, people, plants, and all that moves and breathes within this place. It's not just about the physical space or the geography, it's about the web of spiritual connections binding everything that lives here. There is even a sound in the word that speaks to "concrete knowledge," a knowing that is deeply rooted, something we feel and understand to be true in our bones.

When I learned tmxʷulaxʷ, I was also taught that with this knowledge comes responsibility. We know the names of the mountains and waterways in our language because each place holds stories that tell us how to live in reciprocity with the land, ensuring its regeneration. This isn't just about taking care of the land itself, it's about taking care of all the lives within it, including humans. We have a responsibility to teach others, even those who aren't syilx, how to live within these territories. How else will they know how to behave on these lands, or understand what it means to care for them?

I was taught to be cautious about what we claim rights to. Rights come with responsibilities, and the more rights we claim the more we take on. Our teachings remind us that we aren't just accountable to our own people, we must make sure that all people who live here understand and respect these ways. This isn't something to take lightly, it's about ensuring that everyone knows what it means to live well in these territories, so that tmxʷulaxʷ continues to thrive for all beings who are part of it.

It's important to remember that not everything is appropriation—people taking parts of a culture that don't belong to them for personal gain. Sometimes the pain our people have endured, having been stripped of our identity and displaced from our homelands, makes it hard to see others using or even honouring our knowledge and stories. This pain is real, and it's valid. Yet if we are to move forward, we can't let ourselves be led by fear or the need to control. Healing means learning to act from a place of trust and openness, which must come from within. We need to stay grounded, purpose-driven, and solutions-oriented, especially when we witness others using our teachings in ways that may not align with their original intent.

In 2021 I attended a virtual meeting about water rights. It was hosted by the Okanagan Nation Alliance, with settler partners from various government organizations co-presenting on the topic. These settler presenters began by introducing themselves in nsyilxcen, sharing how they were using syilx knowledge to guide their work around water. For me, this was a powerful example of what it can look like when others work to learn and live by our laws in the territories they reside in. It reminded me that knowledge is meant to support reciprocal relationships and the well-being of all involved, including all living things.

There is no question that some forms of cultural appropriation are harmful. It becomes especially damaging when a dominant culture profits from the knowledge, art, or ceremonies of a marginalized culture without acknowledgment or benefit to that culture. True reciprocity, however, looks different. Sharing our knowledge should be about building mutual understanding, respect, and sustainable relationships with the land and people.

For many of us, sharing knowledge is essential to upholding our laws and way of life. To live in harmony with the land one must understand its original languages, which hold the keys to how we are meant to care for it. If we withhold this knowledge entirely, how can we expect others to respect and live by the natural laws that govern this place?

At the same time it's crucial to reflect on the motivations behind our decisions to share or withhold knowledge. We must ask ourselves: How do I feel about this decision? Am I holding on to knowledge because I believe it gives me an advantage or power? Or am I keeping it with an intention to protect while also practicing and sharing it in a way that strengthens the community and the land? It takes daily work to ensure that our choices come from love and trust rather than fear, control, or a sense of superiority.

I know this isn't easy. After generations of harm there is justified anger and resentment, and a deep sense of injustice. It's hard to watch others gain access to our knowledge without having experienced the same hardships or history. This is why it has taken me decades to find peace in sharing freely. I grew up with very little in the way of material wealth, surrounded by alcoholism, abuse, and the weight of intergenerational trauma. But I also grew up privileged in knowing who I am and where I come from, grounded in my lands, language, teachings, family, and nation.

My name is telxnitk^w, which loosely translates to "standing by water." I come from a line of warriors, the daughter of two strong people and the granddaughter of matriarchs and chiefs who held to our ways. My father, Saul Kenzie Basil, carried a fierce and protective spirit. He was a survivor of residential school, a man who battled his own demons, and he was labelled a militant for his unshakeable belief in our sovereignty and our right to live in accordance with our laws.

He believed that we belonged to the land and answered to no one but the land. He was also a part of the American Indian Movement, standing alongside other Indigenous warriors, including David Dennis's father, in the fight for our people's rights. For him, solidarity among Indigenous nations wasn't just an idea, it was essential to protecting our way of life and honouring our responsibilities to each other.

My mother, Sophie Alec, was a writer, healer, and entrepreneur at heart. She had so much potential within her, dreams for how she could make life better for our people, yet life had worn her down. She didn't always have the confidence to pursue those dreams fully, but she was rooted deeply in our teachings, our culture, and the strength of our language. She raised me with the understanding that our stories, our knowledge, and our ways of seeing the world were powerful and more than enough to guide us. She encouraged me to be open to learning from all beliefs and understandings, and she taught me that while we have our way of knowing, it isn't the only way. When she became sober it marked a turning point for our family, breaking cycles and showing me the resilience that lives within us.

I was raised to trust deeply in the teachings of our people and to stand firm in them. Even in the midst of hardship, surrounded by alcoholism, abuse, and dysfunction, I was given a deep sense of who I am and where I belong. This grounding provided me with a light inside, a steadying force that carried me through dark times. I was raised to believe that, as long as I knew my stories and stayed connected to the land, I would always have a place here no matter what was happening around me. That sense of belonging kept me rooted, reminding me that I was part of something much bigger: my family, my nation, and a lineage of teachings that stretch back to the beginning.

The teachings of our people guide us to remember how to live in respect and reciprocity with all things. They carry the instructions for moving through life's hardest moments with resilience and grace. These stories are gifts meant to be shared to strengthen our spirits and help us and others find a good path forward, no matter how challenging the journey becomes.

It has taken me a long time to say these things out loud. I didn't always feel deserving of claiming space for myself.

Today I am sober, a journey that has been anything but easy. I have moved through pain, loss, joy, and love. I carry the heart and spirit of my ancestors, and I feel their presence as a concrete knowing in my blood. I am a healer, a helper, a warrior. I am the land, I am the water, I am the light. I belong to my people and these lands, and I do not seek permission from anyone outside of my teachings to exist and thrive in this world. I live in a good way, guided by the knowledge passed down by those who came before.

Take a moment to think about these things: Have you allowed yourself to truly feel your pain and trauma, or have you been conditioned to avoid it? What fears come up for you when you consider facing these difficult feelings, and how might embracing them lead you toward a deeper understanding of yourself?

Consider the role of storytelling and ancestral wisdom in your healing journey and self-determination—how can they guide you in living more authentically? If your ancestors come from other lands, take a moment to reflect on the stories, teachings, or practices they might have passed down to help you on your healing journey. What wisdom could be hidden within these stories, waiting to support you in reconnecting with yourself and your heritage? How might embracing these ancestral teachings guide you toward resilience and belonging?

I have been raised to share what I know with those who are open to learning, in order to foster healing. I believe that when we all truly know who we are, we will find within ourselves a deep, unshakable understanding of what it means to be self-determining.

My purpose is to gather and share the knowledge of my ancestors to promote healing for the mind, body, and spirit. I am a storyteller, and it is my responsibility to share.

Chapter 3

HOW DO WE DECOLONIZE?

I never truly understood what colonization meant until I turned forty. I remember a deep conversation with a guy I had just met, Ryan Day. A friend had suggested I reach out to him, saying we might be good supports to each other in the health work we were both involved in. Ryan later became my husband, but I'll never forget the moment when he said, "We are all colonized." I felt a surge of indignation and replied confidently, "I am not colonized. I grew up on the rez with my tema, who spoke the language, and I know our stories." Ryan looked at me with a patience that hinted he understood what I was trying to say, but he also knew that maybe I didn't fully understand what he was trying to tell me. He listened without correcting me or making me feel small, which helped me stay open to what he was trying to share.

Over the next two years I spent time reflecting on my experiences and observing the ways our current systems—both colonial and Indigenous—function. Slowly I came to understand what colonization means in a way that didn't require academic words or jargon to explain.

Colonialism, to me, is built on fear and control, and every system that has grown from it is doing exactly what it was designed to do. Our education, governance, healthcare, and corporate systems are structured on foundations of power, policies, and laws that, knowingly or not, keep people reliant, fearful, and controlled.

These systems were designed not to empower us but to keep us within boundaries set by others, boundaries that disconnect us from our own knowledge, our own authority, and our own ways.

Colonialism isn't just an old concept from history books. It's embedded in the very frameworks that dictate our lives today. And to truly understand it I had to learn to see these structures for what they are, not as neutral systems but as extensions of the same colonial mindset, continually shaping how we view ourselves and each other.

When people are fearful they're working from the brain stem, which means they're only able to use a small fraction of their brain's full capacity—about 5 percent, some say. This part of the brain is all about survival, not creativity or problem-solving. When we're in this state it's almost impossible to think clearly, to find solutions, or to imagine things being different. Fear keeps us stuck, feeling helpless, like we're just doing our best to get by. When we're in survival mode it's easy to settle for the way things are because we don't believe change is possible. That's exactly how systems built on fear and control keep people in line: when people lose hope they're easier to manage.

Studies on the brain have shown us that this isn't just an idea, it's backed by science. The brain stem, which takes over during fear, shuts down our access to higher thinking and locks us in place. For anyone interested in the science behind this, there's research out there that goes deeper into how our brains respond to fear.[2]

When people are fearful, they get stuck. They feel helpless, sure that things can't change, so they settle for the way things are. When we're working from a place of fear we're more likely to stay in the status quo, doing the best we can with what we have, but without hope. And when people lose hope they're easier to control.

---

[2] MacLean, 1973; see also National Library of Medicine

Many of our modern systems are built from fear. When we're afraid, of failure, loss of control, or the unknown, we often look for ways to impose order on the world around us. We try to control the people we live and work with by creating policies, processes, laws, and rigid agendas. We build systems, job descriptions, and operational structures that are so streamlined and standardized that they require little creativity or flexibility to function. In these systems control becomes more valuable than adaptability.

When we look closely at how we work, parent, and build relationships, we start to notice how often we're making decisions from a place of fear. It's anxiety about things going wrong, of not being in control, of things changing. These decisions end up reinforcing colonial systems and structures that prize authority and predictability over connection and creativity.

So how do we decolonize our communities, our lives? Decolonization begins with learning to work from a place of love, trust, and faith in how we work, parent, and build relationships. It requires us to have faith in ourselves and what we know, and it gives us permission to be human beings in a world that has taught us to be perfect performing machines here to do someone else's work. Decolonization means healing ourselves so that we can establish a sense of safety, connection, and belonging in a world that is not safe and connected.

Decolonization calls us to trust in what we know to reclaim our responsibilities through our stories and collective wisdom. This work must be rooted in our traditional teachings, not in written laws or guidelines.

This requires us to reconnect with who we are and where we come from so we can show up as whole, self-determining individuals. Coming-of-age practices and rites of passage are essentially the same journey: they mark the profound transition from one stage of life to another. In many cultures these terms are used interchangeably because they share the same purpose: guiding young people through significant stages of growth.

Coming of Age

For us, coming-of-age isn't just about reaching a certain age, it's a journey that brings us into our teachings, our community, and our responsibilities. Rites of passage are woven into this journey, grounding us in our identity and role within the world. Through these practices we're not just celebrating a new phase of life, we're being rooted in the teachings that make us resilient, in the values that make us strong, and in the knowledge that enables us to walk with self-determination.

These rites are how we heal and reclaim who we are, reminding us of our place within our community, our family, and our land. They are a compass, ensuring that as we move forward we do so with a deep understanding of our responsibilities to ourselves and those around us. At this level of understanding we find the courage to transform systems to align with natural laws that ensure the well-being of all living things and future generations.

In British Columbia we have over 203 First Nations communities. There are 30 different nation languages, but there are close to 60 dialects. I grew up in my mom's nation, the syilx or okanagan nation. We are made up of seven communities in the southern interior of British Columbia that extend into Washington State. Our relatives there are known as the Colville Confederated Tribes. My tema once had land there, and when I was little we would cross the border to dig roots.

Digging roots is done during a specific time of year, and my family members would watch the land for signs to let us know when it was a good time to dig. There are a wide variety of roots that our people dig within our territories. Today many of us gather enough for ceremonies and special gatherings throughout the year, or to give to our elders. It is a long process, and it requires discipline and patience for our families to spend time together and pass on knowledge and stories to foster a sense of connection, belonging, and responsibility. There are things we do while we are on the land to ensure it regenerates: we are careful where and how we dig, and what we put back into the dirt.

Sometimes we had to travel far to find a good place to dig. Many of our digging areas have been damaged by cattle, which compact the ground and make it hard for our roots to thrive and grow. In Canada it often seems that cattle have more rights than Indigenous Peoples. There are a lot of misconceptions about how cattle grazing supposedly benefits the environment. However, policymakers and agricultural industries often overlook the harmful impact this has on our Indigenous food sources and on lands we rely on for ceremony. The practice of taking without giving back has become common, and with it we have forgotten the need to replenish the land for future generations.

> Coyote was given a baby buffalo from the Creator and told, "When you are hungry, you take a little piece of meat, only what you need to eat. If you do this, you will always have food." So each day Coyote would take a little bit of meat from the buffalo, and every night it would regenerate for him. One day Coyote decided he wasn't satisfied with just a little bit of buffalo and, not wanting to feel hungry, ate so much he became stuffed. The baby buffalo did not regenerate and died.

The story of Coyote and the baby buffalo is a powerful teaching about balance and respect for what we are given. Coyote was entrusted with a gift from the Creator and was told, "When you are hungry, take only a little piece of meat, just what you need." If he followed this instruction he would always have food, as the buffalo would regenerate itself. For a while Coyote took only what he needed each day, and every night the buffalo became whole again. But one day he grew impatient and greedy, eating far more than he needed, and the buffalo did not regenerate. It was gone forever.

This story reminds us why we okanagan people do not have buffalo. It is said that Coyote's greed led to its loss. This is a lesson about not taking more than what is needed, about the importance of respecting the limits given by natural law. When we take only what we need things are allowed to regenerate, and we maintain a balance that ensures abundance over time.

Our ancestors knew this well. Each family understood how to care for and regenerate the land they tended to. They planned for each season, choosing different places to hunt, fish, and gather, always careful not to overharvest from one area. They left some behind, knowing that if they respected the land's rhythm it would continue to provide.

We never approached these decisions from a mindset of scarcity. Instead there was a trust, a deep-rooted understanding that by honouring natural law and acting with restraint and respect we would always have enough.

This teaching isn't just about food, it is about our relationships with the land and each other, knowing when enough is enough, and fostering a sense of abundance through careful, mindful interaction with the world around us.

Every year families talked about how and where they would hunt and gather and fish. They talked about the state of the land. Each family would have a representative who let the other family heads know their decisions. The families trusted that the others knew what they were talking about when it came to the area they cared for. They didn't question them or argue with them.

Each of the families contributed to the community in different ways. Some were storytellers, passing on knowledge about the medicines and plants. Some were hunters and knew everything about acquiring meat for the community. Some were helpers, who knew how to take care of someone if they were sick or hurt. Some were good at protecting the community from outside threats. The family heads would come together and talk about what they knew so all the families had the same information and could trust each other, and be able to make good decisions.

This ensured everyone was taken care of. Individuals were raised to know they were loved, that they belonged and had a purpose. When they were confident and knew what their strengths were, without question they were able to contribute to important family discussions. Other family members trusted them because they knew what each other's strengths were. No one in the family was expected to do it all or be everything. Not one person was expected to carry the whole family, because each person in the family was able to contribute.

When each individual contributes to their family, the family functions in a good way and focuses on the work that needs to happen. They will not be fighting against each other, or measuring how much one person is doing or how little, because not everyone is doing the same thing in the same way. Everyone contributes in the way they work best, and everyone trusts that everyone is doing what they need to do.

Our families would come together to make decisions for the community, for the tribe, for the village. In these gatherings everyone contributed to the care of the land, ensuring nothing was overharvested. They knew where to travel and where to set up camp for each season, because they paid close attention and listened to each other with trust. There was no room for ego—no one acted like a know-it-all or tried to control everything. Each person held the same foundational knowledge but brought their unique perspectives and ways of being to the circle.

When we can contribute from our own place of strength and individuality, it gives us a deep sense of pride and confidence, not only in ourselves but in each other. This harmony allows us to love and respect the land in the same way we respect ourselves, our families, our communities, and our nations. When we live this way, trusting in our systems and teachings, the land reciprocates, nourishing us in return.

Coming of Age

Learning to uphold the natural laws of the land was woven into our coming-of-age ceremonies. These teachings were passed down as we spent time on the land, observing it, studying the waters, the plants, and the animals, understanding our place within it all. We were taught to be still, to listen deeply, and to find our role in the regeneration of all living beings.

Each of our nations carries unique responsibilities to the land that are rooted in our stories and language. Our nations span many communities, cities, and regions, yet within each nation are smaller communities known as reserves. Reserves were not a creation of our people, they were imposed by the federal government. Over time many of our families have come to think of themselves as belonging only to a reserve or a single community, but in truth we belong to entire nations. Everywhere our language touches the land is home for us, reminding us that our identity stretches far beyond imposed boundaries.

We didn't try to control how each person contributed, and we didn't expect everyone to be the same. Today, though, there's an unspoken pressure to conform, to fit into a single mould of thinking and behaving. It often feels like blending in has become more important than standing out or staying true to ourselves. We question or push away those who think differently, and we quiet those who don't align with the common way of doing things. When this happens something inside us begins to fade. Our light dims and we become silent, hesitant to be noticed. Over time we lose trust in ourselves and in what we know.

Our leadership often speaks of self-determination, yet we find ourselves caught in cycles that keep us bound to colonial frameworks. In our political spaces, where we talk about sovereignty and reclaiming our authority, too often we're still working from a mindset of fear and scarcity. We end up fighting over land lines and reserve boundaries, as if those divisions truly define us. It's like we're trapped in the same patterns that were imposed on us, relying on colonial legal systems to solve our problems because we're afraid to fully trust in our own stories, our own teachings, and each other.

If we're serious about self-determination, it can't just be a word we use in meetings or a goal on paper. It has to mean trusting that we already have what we need within our own knowledge systems. Self-determination isn't something handed to us by someone else, it's a responsibility to ourselves and to each other. It's about moving beyond reserve boundaries, recognizing that the land itself, not lines on a map, defines who we are. We have to come to the table grounded in the understanding that we are one people connected by our stories, our ancestors, and our shared responsibilities to the land.

True self-determination means being willing to put faith in our own laws, teachings, and wisdom, rather than looking to colonial systems to validate us or to fix what they broke. It means showing up with open hands, not fists, and understanding that the trust we build with each other is what will allow us to break free from the cycles that keep us divided. We have to step away from fear and lean into the strength and resilience that are already part of our identity

When I think about self-determination, I also think about the teachings of people like Gretchen Woodman, who worked with the wet'suwet'en nation to take control of its child welfare system back from the BC government. She believes in bringing innovation in from behind to support tradition, and grounds her work in the wisdom of the body. She reminded me that self-determination is more than just a concept, it's about listening deeply to ourselves, including our bodies, which carry a wisdom that colonial systems have long tried to silence.

Colonial systems have taught us to push through, to work harder, and to measure ourselves by their standards of productivity and success. But true self-determination means reclaiming the power to decide how we define health, balance, and well-being. It's about understanding that rest and care are not signs of weakness but acts of resilience, reconnecting us to our strength and our capacity to show up fully for our communities.

When we stop trying to fit into colonial moulds and start trusting our own ways, we create space for others to do the same. Self-determination means letting go of the fear of how others see us and standing firm in the knowledge that we are enough as we are. It's a commitment to live by our own laws and teachings, grounded in love, trust, and faith, knowing that we are capable of nurturing systems that honour all living things. And in doing so, we step out of cycles of fear and division, building relationships that help us heal and become whole.

Self-determination isn't something we gain from the outside. It's a journey that starts within us, one that asks us to trust ourselves, our stories, and each other. By choosing to live by the wisdom of our ancestors we remember who we are, and we pave the way for future generations to do the same.

The year 2020 forced us all to take a hard look at the world around us. The pandemic separated us from each other and brought our collective fears and vulnerabilities to the surface. We saw the earth responding with fires, floods, and storms, reminders of a climate crisis. People took to the streets, standing up against racial and social inequities that had quietly disrupted lives for generations. The systems the general population was raised to trust, the same ones we depended on for stability, health, and justice, were failing.

In this moment of upheaval, it became clear that spaces of safety, connection, and belonging are essential for us to feel whole. Yet they are rare in a world shaped by fear and control. Many of us found ourselves barely coping, working on the edges of burnout and struggling to keep it together while realizing that the very structures we lived within weren't supporting us in any meaningful way. For me this was a moment of understanding that we can't build lives of belonging or resilience on top of systems that were never meant to hold us.

This brings me back to why decolonization isn't just about resisting oppressive systems, it's about reclaiming our right to be human. It's about remembering our own teachings, our own ways of being that don't require permission from anyone. It's choosing to live in a way that brings us back to love, trust, and connection, not because it's easy, but because it's who we are.

True self-determination is about showing up whole, grounded in our teachings, rooted in our lands, and knowing we belong to something greater than ourselves. It's the strength of being connected to each other, to our ancestors, and to the path ahead.

This journey isn't perfect, and every day I ask myself hard questions. Am I parenting, working, and leading from a place of love? Or am I reacting out of fear? These questions keep me grounded. Decolonization is a daily practice, a choice to show up as a human being, to set down the burden of proving myself within systems that don't truly see me. It's deciding to raise my children and lead my team in a way that centres well-being over achievement, connection over control.

In the end this journey isn't about rejecting everything around us, but about remembering who we are and what we know deep down. It's about coming back to ourselves, to the wisdom in our stories and the resilience in our bones. Decolonization, for me, isn't just about dismantling colonial systems, it's about returning to a way of living that honours connection, compassion, and courage. It's choosing to lead, parent, and work in ways that uplift instead of diminishing, that cultivate belonging rather than isolation.

As I sit with the lessons of these challenging times, I realize that true self-determination is about trust, in ourselves, our communities, and our ancestral teachings. It's about having faith that we can cultivate spaces where we're seen and valued, where our children can grow up knowing they are enough just as they are. It's about making the choice every day to live in a way that reflects the world we want to build, one of love, respect, and kinship.

I invite you to ask yourself the same questions I ask each day: Am I making choices from a place of fear, or am I choosing to trust in the strength and wisdom that's already within me? Am I showing up fully, connected to the land, to others, and to myself? Because in choosing trust and courage over fear, in choosing connection over control, we're doing the work of healing—not just for ourselves but for generations to come. This is the heart of the journey. This is what it means to truly belong.

Chapter 4

IDENTITY

When it comes to good governance and making important decisions, our people were asked two questions before getting to business: "swit askwist" and "stim a spʔus." These two questions could be interpreted as, "Who are you, and what are you doing here?" But if you ever hear a syilx person introduce themselves, they will first introduce themselves and then their parents and grandparents, followed by the lands they come from. This is common practice in many First Nations in British Columbia.

The first question, "swit askwist" (who is your name?) acknowledged the significance of identity when it comes to decision-making. It was essential for you to know who you were and where you came from if you are going to make important decisions for yourself and on behalf of your family, community/nation, and land. When you know who you are and where you come from, you have a sense of identity. You feel belonging and connection, and with that comes a sense of safety. From there you can make good decisions from the best part of your brain.

The second question, "stim a spʔus" (what is on your heart?) acknowledged the importance of your emotions in decision-making. We know we have to be practical with our behaviour so we can be principled in our approach to coexisting with all living things. We know that people can have opposing perspectives, but also that all are needed for us to come together to talk about the problems or issues we need to discuss. This means acknowledging the things on our heart before we get down to business.

The first question helped us centre and regulate so we could work from the best part of ourselves, and the second helped us centre and regulate ourselves as a group. When people shared who they were and what was on their hearts, it connected everyone in the space and helped them build trust, safety, and belonging.

This approach to decision-making is the opposite of what we see in today's workplaces and community centres, where people often introduce themselves only by their names and titles before diving straight into business. When someone's identity is reduced to just their name and job title, it positions them as a role or function, almost like a "perfect performing machine" rather than a whole person. It suggests that their worth and identity are tied to their productivity, rather than to the unique experiences, teachings, and values they bring. This narrow introduction often leads to an environment where people feel pressured to perform and conform, rather than to show up as their true selves.

This can leave people feeling intimidated or uncertain, triggering a reaction based on fear rather than grounded presence. When we feel fearful we work from a survival mode, which can silence us, make us hesitant to share our truths, or encourage us to be overly agreeable just to avoid conflict. In this state we are limited; we're not bringing the full range of our creativity or intelligence to the table. We're just getting through and doing what's expected, not what we're truly capable of.

In our culture, coming-of-age work is deeply tied to identity and belonging. From birth, a child was introduced to the community in nsyilxcen, our language, connecting them to the stories and songs of our people. These stories, songs, and the constant presence of community gave them a strong foundation of identity. They grew up not as isolated individuals but as parts of a larger whole, guided and observed by elders who saw them for who they were and who they could become.

This foundation matters because it nurtures a child's sense of identity and belonging. When they know where they come from and who they are connected to, they feel rooted in something larger than themselves. This sense of belonging isn't just a nice feeling, it's the source of courage and confidence. They're not afraid to speak up or to stand strong in their beliefs because they carry the strength of their ancestors and community within them. Their identity is solid, not something they're constantly questioning or performing.

From this foundation they develop a sense of mastery. They're not just learning skills or knowledge in isolation, they're learning to apply them with purpose and intention, aware of their role in the community and their connection to the land and to each other. Mastery isn't just about competence, it's about understanding how to contribute in a way that benefits the whole. They learn that true mastery comes with the humility to recognize and respect the contributions of others.

When we centre identity and connection, we build communities where people show up as their full selves, grounded and confident. This leads to stronger decisions that reflect a deeper understanding of our collective needs. It fosters environments where people feel safe to speak openly and contribute fully, knowing that their voices are valued. By reinforcing these foundations of identity and belonging we cultivate spaces where courage and mastery are natural outcomes, where people aren't just surviving but thriving together.

When our elders asked "who are you?" they weren't simply seeking a name. They were inviting us, as children, to begin understanding the fullness of who we are and the lineage and land that shaped us. As children this question grounded us, gave us a sense of safety and belonging, and rooted us in something larger than ourselves. It taught us early on that we are connected—to our families, our communities, and the land. This grounding in identity became a foundation we could return to throughout our lives.

As adults this question takes on a deeper meaning. Knowing who we are becomes a source of strength, resilience, and responsibility. It reminds us that true self-determination comes from fully embracing our place within the web of family, community, and land. In a world where we're often reduced to titles and roles, where people are valued for how they perform or conform, this grounded sense of identity becomes a path to courage and authenticity.

To know who we are is to carry the confidence and strength that come from belonging to ourselves, to each other, and to the land. It's a journey that begins as children but continues as adults, allowing us to walk through life connected, unshaken, and ready to contribute from the best part of ourselves. And when we make space for this understanding we cultivate a strength that can't be taken from us—a strength rooted in knowing we belong to something more.

As our gifts began to show themselves our elders would nudge us along, encouraging us to dig deeper into who we were and what we were naturally drawn to. This is what we might call "purpose work" in our coming-of-age practices. Our elders never told us, "This is who you need to be," and we didn't push our children to step into roles just because there was a gap to fill.

If the community needed a healer we didn't force someone into that role if it wasn't their calling. If we needed a leader we didn't place that burden on someone who didn't carry that gift. Instead, each person was encouraged to grow into their own unique strengths, to uncover their path in a way that felt true to them. It wasn't about filling a role, it was about showing up in the way we were meant to. And when everyone could bring their whole selves to the community the gaps filled themselves naturally, because people were living in alignment with their gifts and who they were meant to be.

Identity and purpose work can be a painful journey—not just for Indigenous Peoples but for settler folks who may have lost touch with their own relatives, histories, and traditions. So many people don't know who they are or where they come from, and they have gone most of their lives without knowing their true purpose. For some this disconnection stems from a history of leaving behind homelands marked by war, violence, and hardship.

Many ancestors sought refuge in unfamiliar lands, and in their struggle to survive and blend in they let go of languages, stories, and practices that had once grounded them. Trauma and a desire to start fresh often led to the erasure of family roots, leaving generations adrift, without a sense of belonging to something greater.

Long before colonization, though, many cultures around the world held coming-of-age practices that grounded young people in who they were and connected them deeply to the land and community. These traditions were essential in teaching each generation the values, skills, and responsibilities needed to live with honour and purpose.

In Wales, for instance, storytelling and song were central to passing down wisdom, values, and community history. Boys and girls often gathered in celebrations such as the Eisteddfod, a festival rich with poetry, music, and tales of ancestors and the land. These were not just performances, they were ways to root young people in their history and instill a sense of pride and place. Through these stories they learned the rules of the land and the values that would guide them, ensuring that each new generation carried forward the lessons and strengths of those who came before.

In Scotland, clan society revolved around family loyalty and connection to place. Young men would undergo rites to prepare for adulthood, like hunting or learning to protect the land. They were entrusted with a ceremonial knife, the *sgian-dubh*, symbolizing their readiness to take on responsibility. Alongside practical skills, they were trained in the oral traditions of the clan—the histories and values that bonded them to their community. These practices weren't just survival tactics, they were about grounding young people in a shared identity and purpose, ensuring that each person knew their place within a greater whole.

Similarly, in Ireland, coming-of-age rites emphasized connection to the land and to each other. Young men and women participated in ceremonies filled with songs and blessings, rituals that spoke to both strength and care, qualities they would need as adults. They were taught their family's lineage, the significance of the land, and the values they were expected to carry forward. This wasn't merely a transition into adulthood, it was a commitment to upholding the ties that bound them to their ancestors and the land itself.

These practices across cultures were not just about moving from childhood to adulthood, they were about rooting each person in a story, a purpose, and a collective responsibility. Colonization disrupted and erased many of these traditions, pulling people away from their own paths and into systems that didn't honour individuality, community, or connection. The loss of these rites left many adrift, disconnected from their roots and purpose and unsure of where they belonged.

Reclaiming these roots—whether Indigenous or settler—is about rebuilding that sense of belonging and purpose. It's about remembering that we all come from rich, interconnected histories, and that we each have stories, strengths, and responsibilities to carry forward. Finding our way back to who we are, and honouring the journeys of our ancestors, allows us to create a foundation of identity and purpose not just for ourselves, but for the generations to come. It's about stepping into a way of life that honours connection, courage, and care, qualities that are part of us and waiting to be reclaimed.

For many settlers disconnection from their roots was a choice, an escape from hard lives, poverty, conflict, and trauma in the lands they left behind. Families arrived on these shores with dreams of starting over, often distancing themselves from their pasts and the difficult stories they couldn't bear to pass on.

But for us as Indigenous Peoples, that disconnection wasn't chosen. It was forced upon us through colonial policies and actions that systematically tore apart our families, communities, and relationship to the land. We come from cultures with protocols and ways of being that ensured everyone was cared for, no matter the circumstances.

Before colonization we had systems of responsibility embedded in our kinship practices. If a woman lost her husband, his brother would care for her and her children. If there was no family nearby, the children would often be sent to live with relatives elsewhere in the territory, sometimes miles away. Our sense of family wasn't limited to blood alone, it was woven into our collective responsibility, a deep understanding that we all belonged to one another.

But when colonization took hold this natural web of care and connection was systematically torn apart. Our people were forced onto reservations, plots of land that were far from where we were meant to be and not meant to sustain us, and we couldn't leave without a written pass from the local Indian agent.

Alcohol was introduced to us, a substance that became a tool of further disruption and control. Then came the residential schools, institutions designed to sever our children from their language, their culture, and their families. This kind of forced separation fractured our communities. Trauma spread, alcoholism took root, and internal violence grew. There are countless stories of affairs, rapes, and even incest, resulting in children born into silence, their origins hidden in shame. Families fractured further as these difficult histories went unspoken. The weight of trauma was passed down through generations, held quietly behind closed doors.

Today many of us, Indigenous and settler alike, face the struggle of reconnecting with families, communities, and histories fragmented by generations of displacement, silence, and shame.

For some Indigenous Peoples these breaks in connection were created by adoptions, colonial violence, and stories too painful to share. Families were often separated, children raised by relatives without clear lineage, and some connections blurred by secrets born from trauma. Within these stories lie the heartaches of disconnection, the lost threads of family lines, and the complexities of healing from silence that has kept people from truly knowing who they are.

But healing is happening. In our communities people are beginning to speak openly about histories once buried in shame, releasing the silence that weighed us down. This process isn't about holding on to the pain but letting go of shame that never belonged to us. Through this journey we are reshaping what it means to belong, not just to a family or a community but to a history that we are now strong enough to hold and to heal.

Reclaiming these roots is about creating a world where we belong not just to ourselves, but to each other and to the land. For us, this work involves undoing the erasure of our traditions, rediscovering the protocols and roles that sustained our communities and returning to practices of reciprocity and balance. Reclaiming our stories is about finding our way back to who we are, reconnecting with the resilience in our bones and stepping forward with a new understanding of where we come from and who we're meant to be. This isn't just a personal journey, it's one that reshapes our families, our communities, and our collective future so that the generations to come will grow up knowing they are part of something greater that is deeply rooted, and that they belong.

As a child I learned the importance of talking about our lineage and who our families were. Knowing who we were and where we came from kept us connected. We knew our histories and accepted the choices our families made around adoptions or relationships, even when some stories held pain. I could sense when a difficult memory surfaced by the way adults would grow quiet or quickly shift the conversation. These silences revealed stories that were too heavy to carry out loud.

My tema taught me that knowing who you are is powerful. When I was a little girl I experienced an incredible amount of racism from other kids, but my tema would tell me to feel sorry for them. She'd say that we didn't know what was going on in their homes that made them act that way. It was her way of helping me see that their cruelty came from somewhere deeper: a place of pain or confusion. She also taught me that racism, at its root, was often about people not knowing who they were. She would remind me, "Feel sorry for them, because they probably don't know who they are or where they come from. But you do."

My mom added to that teaching, explaining that people who don't know who they are don't have a sense of true identity. She would say that they're like dust in the wind, "whizzing around in space, lost and confused." Without roots, without a sense of belonging, they can feel threatened or empty inside, and that's when they turn to violence, hurtful words, or judgment to feel powerful. It's as if they're trying to take from others to fill a void within themselves.

My tema and mom wanted me to understand that knowing who you are—your lineage, your place in the world, and the values you carry—is a shield against this kind of emptiness. When you're grounded in your identity you don't need to hurt others or tear them down, because you're steady in yourself. My tema's teaching was a reminder that those kids' actions didn't define me—they were reflections of something unhealed in them. She taught me that by holding on to my identity I was protecting myself from being pulled down by their hurt or hate.

For my mom, identity wasn't just a source of confidence, it was a kind of power that didn't rely on anyone else's approval or validation. When people know who they are, they have courage and a healthy sense of their own power so they don't feel the need to take it from others. But those who lack this grounding may try to assert themselves by pushing others down, reacting out of insecurity rather than strength.

Their teachings shaped the way I saw the world. They helped me understand that identity isn't just something personal, it's a foundation. It gives you a way to respond to the world with dignity and compassion, even when others don't treat you with the same. When you know who you are, you're connected to something greater. Your ancestors, your land, the stories that shaped you, and this connection can help you weather the harshest storms.

My tema and mom taught me that identity is both an anchor and a shield, and that no one's actions could ever take mine away from me. It is essential for all of us to remember who we are and where we come from because each of us has gifts to share. How deeply do you know your own identity and lineage? In what ways has your understanding of who you are and where you come from shaped your choices, relationships, and sense of purpose?

Reflect on the practices, stories, or values that connect you to your ancestors or heritage. Are there teachings that help you stay grounded? How might reconnecting with these aspects of your identity strengthen your sense of belonging, connection, and confidence as you navigate the world?

Remember, the journey of identity is not simply about knowing who you are, it's about cultivating the courage to live in alignment with that knowledge. In embracing our lineage and reclaiming the stories and strengths that belong to us, we find the courage, confidence, and belonging to show up fully in the world—not just for ourselves, but for each other.

Chapter 5

THE FOUR SIBLINGS

In the beginning there were four siblings from each of the four races who all lived on the same land. In our stories we have always talked about the siblings and four colours like the medicine wheel: black, red, white, and yellow. When our elders told these stories, they did not share or reference the colours of the races in a derogatory way. They have shared these teachings for decades to talk about our relationships to each other and to remind us that we are all relatives.

Each of the siblings was given a gift they were supposed to master. The Creator told the siblings, "You must master these gifts. When you come back together again you will teach each other what you have mastered, and you will listen to each other and learn and the world will be good. If you do not share your gifts and keep them to yourselves, or if you do not listen to each other, there will be war."

The Creator gave each of the siblings a teaching. Some of our nations say the Creator gave each of the siblings a tablet with instructions, and that those tablets are still out there. These tablets carry the original teachings that were meant to be shared with each other so they could live in peace on earth together. They were told that if even one of them forgot those teachings or cast them to the side, all humans would suffer and the earth would die. These teachings or tablets are said to be in Arizona, Tibet, Switzerland, and Mount Kenya.

The black sibling was given the gift of water. They were told that even in the desert they would be able to find water and know how to harness its power. The yellow sibling was given the gift of air and told that they would be able to harness its power for discipline and strength. The white sibling was given the gift of fire and told that they would harness its power to use it create things like engines and machines. The red sibling was given the gift of land and told that they would learn everything about it and its natural law, and they would know everything about regenerating it.

The Creator told the four siblings that they would now be sent into the four directions to master their gifts, and that what separated them would be what brought them back together again. The Creator struck the land with a wooden stick. It began to crack and separate, and water came up between the cracks. It would be this water that would bring them back together again.

Our prophecies speak of a time when the four siblings would reunite, drawn back to one another through the power of memory and teachings. But as they separated into the four directions, they began to forget. In their forgetfulness, war and division took root and a period known in our stories as the "hundred years of darkness" began. This darkness spread as humans lost connection to their true purpose, each sibling forgetting their own gift and what it was meant to bring to the circle.

Our elders tell us that this doesn't have to be our fate. They remind us that we are given many chances to remember, to come back to the teachings we were given and to find each other again. But this requires a kind of listening that isn't always easy. It means opening our hearts to our shared stories, to the truths we may have been avoiding, and to the wisdom that has been held for us all this time.

For so long these stories and teachings were kept quiet. Many misunderstood this silence as secrecy, thinking that only certain people were allowed to know them, or that they were reserved exclusively for Indigenous ears. But in truth the stories were waiting for the right moment, for those who would listen deeply and take responsibility for what they learned.

The elders and storytellers have always been ready, patient, waiting for a time when we could collectively hold these stories with the respect and care they deserve.

Now, in the spirit of the four siblings, we are invited to look beyond our differences, to recognize each other as relatives and see that each of us has something vital to offer. This isn't just a call to remember our original teachings, it's an invitation to step forward with respect, compassion, and a willingness to share. Healing and unity require both individual mastery and collective responsibility. We each have our own work to do, but we are not meant to do it alone.

The Invitation to Heal

The next part of this chapter holds stories of resilience in the face of immense hardship: the accounts of those who endured the experience of residential schools. These stories carry the weight of trauma but also reveal the incredible strength it took to survive. As you read these accounts I invite you to take a deep breath, ground yourself in where you are, and remember that you are safe in this moment.

These stories are shared to bring truth to light, to honour those who lived through this history and to guide us toward a future where such suffering has no place in our legacy. At any point, if these stories feel overwhelming it's okay to pause, to hold space for your feelings, and to come back to them when you're ready. This is all part of our journey to understanding, healing, and reconnecting with the teachings of the four siblings. Together we are reclaiming a path forward that honours every voice, every story, and every gift in the circle.

Our elders held our stories in silence, not because they wanted to but because survival sometimes means keeping parts of ourselves hidden. Canada's government used every tool it had to sever our connection to who we were, hoping we'd forget. It wasn't just about taking our land—though that was part of it—it was about taking the essence of who we were as Indigenous peoples, taking our teachings, our language, our ceremonies, and, most unforgivably, our children.

In the late 1800s they pushed us onto reservations, managing us through Indian agents who controlled every aspect of our lives. The government partnered with churches to open residential schools all over the country. And then they created the RCMP, a force dedicated to ensuring we stayed where we were told, silencing our gatherings, our ceremonies, our very way of being together. They made it illegal for us to gather so our people held ceremonies in the dark, with doors and windows covered.

The first Indian residential school opened in 1831, and over the next century more than 130 schools spread across the country. These places were not schools in the way we think of learning, they were institutions built to strip us of our culture and, ultimately, of ourselves. Children, some as young as three, were taken and never came home. Parents tried to hide their children to keep their families together, but year after year they were stolen away. Some stayed at the schools fourteen years or more, losing the warmth of family, the comfort of language, and the security of knowing where they belonged.

They took our children, packed them into cattle trucks like livestock, and drove them away from their families, their homes, their land. The government chose this way because it was cheap and cruelly efficient. They could fit as many of our children as possible into those cold metal trailers, treating them as though they were something less than human, something that could be herded and shipped. Loading them into cattle trucks was a deliberate attempt to break something sacred, to reduce them to numbers, to bodies. It was the beginning of a brutal process that aimed to sever our children from who they were, from the language, stories, and ceremonies that grounded them in the world.

Those cattle trucks were meant to dehumanize them, to strip away their belonging and sense of self. But those efforts failed. Though scarred and hurt, they carried fragments of their identity with them. And today, as we reclaim our language, our ceremonies, and our connections to each other, we honour that resilience. We stand strong in the knowledge that our land, our language, and our ceremonies were never lost. They endured within our ancestors even in the darkest times, and because of that they continue to live within us.

For those who couldn't hide their children there was the quiet hope that they'd see them again over the holidays, if they could somehow gather enough money to make the trip. Others turned to hiding them with relatives far from the schools, hoping distance would keep them safe. But as Indian day schools opened in communities, they pulled our children even deeper into the system. These schools may have allowed children to return home at night, but they followed the same blueprint of stripping us of our identity and culture. They were part of the same machine, turning the wheels of assimilation in every corner of our lives.

The hunger that haunts our elders is a story in itself. Children in those schools were starved, not just of food but of care, of kindness, of the basic needs that let a child feel safe. I've heard so many stories of children sneaking out, stealing food, raiding orchards just to ease the hunger gnawing at them. And this deprivation wasn't just from neglect, it was calculated. In the 1940s and 1950s government-sanctioned researchers began using our children for nutritional experiments. They treated them like subjects in a lab, withholding vitamins, nutrients, basic food, to see what would happen.

This wasn't hidden research. It was done with the full knowledge of those in power. No one asked permission, no one thought of the children as human beings with voices and families. School staff were instructed not to give them what they needed, to let them suffer in silence so they could study the effects. Those children were robbed of their health, their dignity, and even their humanity, all in the name of so-called science.

Leaving those schools, our elders were left with the kinds of wounds that don't heal easily. Many left with a relationship to food that would haunt them, a need to eat whenever they could, as much as they could, because they'd learned that food could disappear. It became survival instinct—a deep-seated need to never feel hungry again, to never feel that hollowness that the schools had forced upon them.

This fear of scarcity, this drive to eat more than needed, planted roots deep within them, and we see its effects in our communities today. Diabetes, obesity, heart disease—these health issues aren't just statistics. They're the legacy of a system that used food as a weapon against us.

And even now, generations later, many of us still carry that fear, that urgency around food. It shows up in how we eat, in the need to stockpile, in the sense of unease when resources feel scarce. We see our elders, our parents, and ourselves struggling with this unspoken legacy, this trauma around something as basic as eating.

But it's more than just the food, more than the health struggles. This hunger, this deprivation, disconnected us from the way our ancestors understood food. We were once guided by teachings that showed us how to honour the land, how to harvest and share in a way that left plenty for those who came next. Food wasn't just nourishment, it was ceremony, it was gratitude, it was relationship. The schools took that relationship from us, turning food into something we had to fight for, something that was given or withheld to control us.

The children endured punishments so severe that I have a hard time writing this. They are things I've heard from my elders and those who survived, but it has taken me a long time to put them on paper. Priests and nuns sometimes beat them until bones broke and blood spilled, and some children were beaten so mercilessly they didn't survive. Those who were brave enough to speak their language, a simple act of remembering who they were, were whipped or even had their tongues burned. Young girls who became pregnant by the priests were forced to hide their pregnancies, and when they gave birth their babies were stolen from them, sometimes drowned in nearby rivers or burned in the basements. Children ran away to escape these horrors but many never made it home, some dying by suicide or succumbing to the unforgiving elements, their young lives cut short by an unforgiving system.

When children finally did return home they came with a deep, ingrained terror of punishment. It wasn't a generic fear, it was the result of brutal, calculated violence. Years of beatings and abuse left them instinctively bracing for the worst, afraid that any slip, any sign of their identity, could bring punishment down upon them again.

This fear was so powerful it shaped not only their time at the schools but the way they would carry themselves once they left. Some of them lost their language entirely. Those who managed to hold on to it often chose not to pass it on. They hid their teachings, shielding their own children and grandchildren from the risk of experiencing that same violence. They thought silence was safer, that maybe if the next generation learned only colonial ways, if they could excel in settler education, they could avoid the horrors they'd endured and somehow thrive in the world that was being forced upon them.

In residential schools our children were taught to despise everything that made them who they were. They were told they were dirty, ugly, and even evil; They were called "devil." They were forced to abandon their own spirituality and embrace Christianity, whether Catholicism or Protestantism, because it was supposed to "save" them. They were shamed into believing that their parents and their ways were heathen, that their songs, dances, and ceremonies were wicked and had to be left behind. This was part of the larger goal of residential schools: to strip us of our culture, to erase our identities, to force us to become something we were not.

I think of elders who have shared that, as children, they didn't understand why they were taken. No one explained it to them. Many thought their parents no longer wanted them or had given them away. They internalized a sense of being bad or unworthy, of being unlovable. The very moment they were taken their sense of belonging, of being wanted, was shattered. When some finally returned home they didn't even recognize their own parents, and many parents didn't recognize their own kids.

Our elders remember life before the schools: being on the land, gathering and hunting, and laughing with their families. They remember the warmth of their parents' smiles, the shared work, the joy. But when they came home after their time at the schools their parents were changed. Before, they had taken pride in their appearance, kept their hair long, wore clothing that reflected their culture. Now they dressed like settlers, their hair cut short, and many looked worn down and dirty. The sparkle in their eyes was gone, replaced with anger and pain, with the numbness that comes from surviving too much. Alcohol often filled the void left by loss and loneliness.

The government's intention was clear: "Kill the Indian in the child." The moment children arrived at the schools they were scrubbed with scalding water, and their hair was cut to strip them of any connection to their identity. They were forbidden from speaking their language, and any slip led to brutal punishment.

The depth of our teachings, our traditions, was often passed on by the water's edge, a sacred space for us. But even our waters were taken from us, diverted to feed settler communities and ranches, which left our lands and traditions parched. And yet our stories endured, whispered in quiet gatherings, shared in hushed voices, protected for future generations.

Our people held on to them not just for ourselves, but for the sake of all living beings—humans, yes, but also plants, animals, water. My mom's nation speaks of egalitarian law, a belief that every living thing has a voice, and that with voice comes responsibility. As people with the ability to speak, we carry the duty to protect and speak for those who cannot: the animals, the water, the plants, even the smallest insects.

These stories, teachings, and ways of knowing have survived not because they were written down, but because they were lived, protected, and passed on. They are gifts from our ancestors, carried forward so that we can live in balance and reciprocity. As we remember them, we reclaim not only our past but our responsibility to the land, to each other, and to all beings.

There's a brutal legacy here, a calculated attempt to erase who we are and break every bond that tied us to our land, our language, and each other. This isn't just a story of trauma, it's a living memory, a wound that still pulses in our families and communities. But it's also a story of resilience, of a strength that was forged in that unimaginable pain. Because even as they tried to strip us down, they couldn't take it all.

Our identity survived, carried in our blood and held on to through generations of our people who refused to forget. Our stories, our ceremonies, our connection to the land endured. And that endurance, that persistence, is our power. It's a reminder that no matter how hard they tried to erase us, we're still here, reclaiming, healing, and finding our way back to ourselves.

In November 2012, a protest movement called #IdleNoMore was started in Saskatoon by four women: three First Nations and one non-Indigenous ally. It is a grassroots movement among First Nations, Métis, and Inuit peoples across Canada that was inspired by the introduction of omnibus bill C-45, the "Jobs and Growth Act," by the Parliament of Canada, which included measures that weakened environmental protections laws. In response, Attawapiskat Nation Chief Theresa Spence began a six-week liquid-diet hunger strike in Northern Ontario in December 2012.

The movement was supported by non-Indigenous allies across Canada and other parts of the world, and was coordinated through social media to bring attention the legislative abuses of Indigenous Peoples by Stephen Harper's Conservative government.

An omnibus bill is tabled when the government tries to pass a number of bills that cover diverse and unrelated topics in hopes of passing them all in one motion, instead of going through each bill individually. They are often used to pass controversial amendments.

Our nations and the Canadian system of reserves has been governed since 1876 by the Indian Act, which dictates our people's land use, governance, education, and healthcare, among many other things. Bill C-45 includes legislation that impacts the Indian Act in voting and approval procedures for proposed land designations. It made technical amendments to the Canadian Environmental Assessment Act, and to the Navigable Waters Protection Act which removed thousands of lakes and streams from federal protection under that law. The Conservatives said the changes streamlined regulations and removed red tape that held up projects along waterways that "impeded navigation." However, they also removed the environmental oversight of some of Canada's most treasured lakes and rivers.

Sometime near the end of December 2012, I hosted an Idle No More meeting at the Penticton Indian Band community hall to find out how we could support the movement. We talked about holding education and storytelling sessions at the Penticton Library and Museum and drumming and singing sessions at

Cherry Lane shopping mall. At that meeting we talked about what was happening around the world, about allies from all over the world stepping up to support Indigenous Peoples.

It was during that time that our ceremonial people, our medicine-bundle holders, our prophecy- and storytellers started to share our teachings publicly. They talked about warriors of all races and colours coming together to fight for the land and water, for Mother Earth.

Our prophecy people said, "Now is the time our medicine and knowledge will be picked up by young people. For so long, it was only the old people who carried medicine and bundles and pipes, but more and more young people will wake up to their gifts and knowledge and responsibilities."

We started to share the stories of our four siblings again. Fighting Bill C-45 was about protecting the water. It was the water that brought us back together again. It was a time of awakening. It was told that we were coming out of the hundred years of darkness and remembering our stories. Now that people were ready to listen, it was time for our storytellers to start sharing their teachings. More importantly, it was time for us to start remembering who we are and our water teachings.

Idle No More started a revolution, waking many of us up to step into our roles and acknowledge who we are, and since then Indigenous Peoples have started to focus on mastering our gifts, remembering who we are and reclaiming our spaces, opening them up to be seen.

Nine years after the Idle No More movement began, our world was shaken. In June 2021, in BC's southern interior, the remains of 215 Indigenous children were found in unmarked graves in tk'emlúps te secwépemc First Nation territory on the grounds of the former Kamloops Indian residential school. Since then the world has begun to learn about the atrocities that have been happening to Indigenous Peoples since the government of Canada arrived with the intent to "kill the Indian in the child." Duncan

Campbell Scott, deputy superintendent of the Department of Indian Affairs from 1913 to 1932, made the following egregious claim in 1920, before the amendment to the Indian Act became law that same year:

> I want to get rid of the Indian problem. I do not think as a matter of fact, that this country ought to continuously protect a class of people who are able to stand alone. That is my whole point . . . Our object is to continue until there is not a single Indian in Canada that has not been absorbed into the body politic, and there is no Indian question, and no Indian department, that is the whole object of this Bill.

The centennial of this bill, coupled with the horrific scene at the Kamloops Indian residential school, has Canadians from all backgrounds wanting to listen to and learn from the experiences of Indigenous Peoples in Canada. There is nationwide discussions now about decolonization, about dismantling systemic racism and overturning policy that is deeply imbedded into every government, corporation, and institution in the country.

Our prophecies have always told us that nothing happens by accident, that we're exactly where we're meant to be in this moment, hearing and seeing what we're meant to. The Four Siblings Prophecy spoke of a hundred years of darkness, a time that would push us so far from our original teachings that we'd forget we are all connected, all relatives.

That time of darkness came, and its pain was carved into our people through the horror of residential schools. Our children were taken from us and their identities stripped, their hearts and minds battered by a system determined to silence them. This suffering wasn't just a wound to the individuals who endured it, it tore at the entire web of our people, unravelling the very fabric that held us together.

Yet even in our darkest times, our teachings remained. The prophecy told us there would be a way back, that this disconnection wasn't the end of our story. To find that way back we have to remember who we are, where we come from, and, most importantly, that we're meant to walk together. The Idle No More movement was a call to action that stirred something ancient within us, a reminder that we carry the strength and teachings to stand together, to lift each other up, to reclaim our voices.

And so we tell these stories, not just to remember the pain, but to heal through it and find our way back to each other. It's time to learn from each other again, to reconnect with our sense of identity and belonging so that we can move forward with confidence and strength. This is our responsibility—not just to ourselves, but to all living things.

Take a moment to reflect on what these teachings mean in your own life.

How do you connect with your own story, your own identity, and the journey that brought you here? Are there parts of your past, or the history of your family or community, that you feel called to remember and heal?

Think about the ways fear and control might shape the systems around you, and consider how love, trust, and a sense of interconnectedness could offer a different way forward. How might you approach your decisions or relationships differently if they were grounded in those values?

The Four Siblings Prophecy speaks of a way back to unity and balance after a time of darkness. In your own life, are there relationships or connections that you feel ready to heal, to bring closer, or to see with new eyes?

As we walk on this path of healing, how can you begin to tell and live your story in a way that uplifts others and strengthens community?

These questions aren't just for Indigenous people, they're for everyone who feels the pull to reconnect with a deeper sense of belonging and purpose. Our stories are pathways to understanding who we are and how we're connected. Where might this reflection lead you in your own journey?

This path forward requires love and trust, not fear and control. It requires that we see ourselves and each other through the lens of our teachings. That is true self-determination, a journey we can only make by walking the path of healing together. These stories are our instructions, not just for Indigenous Peoples but for everyone willing to learn. They hold a map to a life of balance, courage, and connection for all of us.

As you close this chapter, take a moment to ground yourself in the present. Look around, feel the space you're in, and breathe deeply, allowing yourself to come back from these stories and reflect on what they mean to you.

Navigating the pain of these injustices and the weight of our shared history can feel overwhelming. But remember, this journey through our stories, our teachings, and our prophecies is not just about acknowledging the darkness we've endured, it's about reigniting the hope that carries us forward. Our stories hold the power to heal, to remind us of our connection, and to guide us back to balance and belonging.

Let these teachings remind you that, despite everything, we are still here, moving forward together. How will you take this sense of hope into your next steps? What will you carry forward from these stories, and how might they shape the way you walk in this world?

Now is the time to remember. Now is the time to tell these stories.

Chapter 6

BUCKSKIN TIES

Growing up, I learned that coming-of-age wasn't just about reaching a certain age. It was about understanding who we are, where we come from, and the responsibilities we carry. My tema and mom brought me to community gatherings, where our people would meet to discuss issues that mattered to us. They weren't worried about whether I'd understand every word. They knew that just being there, feeling the strength in the room and soaking in the voices of our elders, would shape me in ways words couldn't explain.

I remember those times vividly: the smell of food cooking in the band hall's kitchen and the paintings on the walls, each one a reminder of our stories. There was a hum in the air, a mix of laughter and serious voices, and the warmth of our language flowing through the room. My tema would sit among the other elders, her face calm and strong as she listened deeply. I'd sit beside her, my legs dangling off the bench, trying to keep still as I absorbed everything around me.

Those gatherings were about more than business, they were about staying connected, remembering who we are. Every person there had a role. The elders listened until it was their time to speak, and when they did the room quieted to absorb their words. They weren't just talking about land rights, housing, or policies, they were grounding us in our teachings, reminding us to not get lost in agreements that didn't honour our ways. Every word they shared was woven with generations of knowledge, carrying the weight of teachings meant to guide and protect us.

Looking back I see that those gatherings were my first lessons in self-determination. My tema and mom understood that I didn't need to grasp every detail to understand the importance of what was happening. Just being there taught me to listen—not just with my ears, but with my heart—to feel the weight of what was unsaid as much as what was spoken. Our people have always learned this way, through watching, listening, feeling.

Our people gathered in those rooms to remind themselves who they were, to hold on to their identity, meeting by meeting, even when the outside world tried to make them forget. This was our coming-of-age, our path to becoming who we were meant to be—not by following a set path, but by finding our way back to ourselves, our families, and our land.

True leadership, I learned from watching them, isn't about power or position. It's about connection. It's about listening to your people, your land, your teachings, and remembering that every decision touches generations to come. My tema and the elders never said this outright but I felt it in their presence, in the respect they showed each voice, in the way they carried our teachings forward.

One thing I remember clearly is the way they respected each other. No one ever spoke over another, and no one raised their voice in anger. When they were stern it was with a weight that didn't need shouting to be heard. And when they spoke in our language it felt like the air itself held still to listen. The language carried a power rooted in our connection to the land and our ancestors. Speaking in our language wasn't just communication, it was a reminder of our shared history and our place in it.

They didn't need to dominate the conversation because they knew true strength was in listening, in respecting each voice. Each person trusted that their turn would come, that their words would be heard in their fullness. Watching them I learned that real power doesn't need to prove itself, it simply is. Like the roots of a tree, it is quiet but unwavering, drawing its strength from the land it's anchored in.

For them, it was essential to weave our stories into everything we did, whether it was negotiating with the government, discussing land rights, or planning business developments. Our stories weren't just remnants of the past, they were the foundation of every decision. They reminded us of our values, of the land we came from, and of the responsibility we carried forward.

In those meetings, our stories kept us grounded. They brought context to every conversation, reminding us that our decisions weren't just about today but about those who came before us and those who would come after. Our language and stories were like a compass, anchoring us in our syilx identity, reminding us of truths that colonial frameworks could never encompass.

Even in the most modern negotiations, our stories asserted our identity. Bringing them into those spaces wasn't just tradition, it was a form of resistance, a way to claim space in a world that often tried to erase us. It was our way of saying, *We are still here, and our ways of knowing and being still matter.*

By the mid-eighties we began to confront the realities of alcoholism and drug use in our communities. The first person in our community recognized for getting sober was Louise Gabriel, the matriarch of a large family who took on emergency response, health, and social services roles in our community. Although I don't know the exact year Louise chose to get sober—perhaps it was in the 1970s—her decision marked a powerful turning point for many in our community. Louise was a true leader, a woman ahead of her time who was passionate about the well-being of children and families. She served as an elected council member at a time when few women were on council, and her strength was evident in her commitment to her people.

Coming of Age

Louise's sobriety was more than a personal journey, it was a symbol of resilience and strength, inspiring others to take a similar path. She was known not only for her service roles but for her bold actions. She participated in a government-building takeover at the Department of Indian Affairs, where the news labelled her and others, including other elders, as "hotheads," but to our people she was a voice for justice. She also had a vision to bring back our traditional dugout canoes and organize a unity paddle across the border, reconnecting our people separated by the American-Canadian divide.

Years later the ripple effect of her influence became clear as more community members, now in their forties, including my mom, left to attend treatment centres in Vernon and Prince George, BC, the closest available facilities. Louise's example had sown seeds of change, inspiring our community to start thinking about wellness in a different way. As more of our people took responsibility for their health, conversations opened about how to create a better future for our children. Louise's influence extended beyond her own family—she always made time to talk with me, sharing insights that went deeper than words. Her journey was a reminder of the power in reclaiming our well-being, not only for ourselves but for the generations that would come after us.

Around this time I was only a child, about nine or ten years old, but I began to hear our elders talk about the importance of coming-of-age ceremonies and rites of passage. They knew that bringing back these practices would ground us in identity, connection, and belonging. With a strong sense of who we are, we carry an inner power that no one can take from us. And with that power we're no longer driven to take it from others through violence, whether in words or actions.

The adults in our community began working with our elders to hold camps for young people. These weren't just ordinary gatherings, they were organized to root us in our identity and teachings. Kids of different ages were invited to gather at Owl

Rock, a place steeped in our stories located by a lake where, according to our teachings, a giant turtle lived at its bottom. Above the lake was an area where our people went to fast, a sacred place for reconnecting with ourselves and the spirit world.

These camps became our way of returning to what grounded us, strengthening our spirits, and teaching us resilience in ways that would shape us for life, reconnecting with ourselves. There were the remnants of an underground house there, a structure dug deep into the earth that kept people warm in winter and cool in summer, and a longhouse where stories, ceremonies, and teachings were shared.

We'd set up our tents and the adults would guide us, sharing stories and taking us onto the land to learn about the medicines and plants. Sometimes they'd take us hunting and we'd learn how to skin and butcher deer, respecting each part of the animal. Before dawn each day someone would walk through the camp, beating a drum to wake us up. We'd stumble out of our tents, groggy but determined and run down to the lake. The cold water would wake us up, then we'd race back to camp refreshed and ready for the day's teachings.

We were never told why we did these things. There wasn't an explanation about how running or swimming would build resilience or discipline. We just followed. It was the same back in the community. Some adults were known for instilling discipline, often picking kids up from their homes to take them swimming or making them run laps. Behind my tema's house there was a hill that we were often sent up when we got restless, and we'd climb it without question.

I remember how I'd push myself even when my legs were burning or the water felt like ice. No one yelled or forced us to keep going. But there was a quiet encouragement in the way they watched us, an expectation that we'd push past our limits. I didn't realize it then, but each time I pushed myself I was building something inside. I was strengthening not just my body but my mind and spirit, learning to trust my own endurance, my own resilience.

When we were on the land it was never just about being outdoors, it was about presence and respect. We were told to move quietly, to pay attention. To avoid startling the spirits we'd put soot on our faces, a simple ritual that reminded us to walk with respect. We were told to say our Indian names aloud so the land would recognize us and care for us. We'd put water in our mouths and spray it into the air, a greeting to the land and the spirits, a way of saying, *We're here!*

Every act we performed connected us to the land, grounding us in the knowledge that we belonged there. And every time we pushed past discomfort, whether it was the chill of the lake or the ache in our legs, we were nurturing more than just physical strength, we were developing the mental and spiritual resilience that would carry us through life's challenges.

Today I see so many of us struggling with confidence and discipline. We live in a world that teaches us to work from a place of fear. We hold on tightly to control, thinking it will protect us, make us feel safe. But in those camps we learned a different kind of strength. We learned that resilience isn't about rigid control, it's about trust, discipline, and connection.

Those camps weren't just about survival or testing our endurance, they were about cultivating a quiet confidence in ourselves and in the land. We learned that we belonged, that we were part of something much greater than ourselves, something that would hold us and support us if we remembered how to listen and connect. That's what we took away from those experiences—not just a skill or a memory, but a foundation of belonging that still runs deep in our veins.

Working from fear and control freezes us. When we hear things like "we need to do coming-of-age ceremonies," our first response is to try to figure out what that means. We want to know everything about it before we do anything. We want to know what it is, why it is, what the original purpose was, and how it was done. How can we do it today in a way that makes sense to us? When things make sense and are laid out by steps in front of us, we feel we can trust them.

Ancestral wisdom and knowledge came from observing natural law passed down through storytelling and action. Many of our elders remind us that teachings and language cannot be absorbed in a classroom, they have to be lived. Just reading about something won't give you what you need for it to become a part of you. Our way of teaching is experiential, allowing us to apply concepts in real-world settings and value mistakes as steps toward understanding.

We were taught that you can't figure things out just by standing around and talking, you have to start moving. There's a time to listen to the stories and a time to act, even if you don't fully understand where it will lead. When you start doing, the emotions you feel from that experience help deepen your understanding and make the knowledge stick.

I was once told that "overthinking is under-feeling." Our people have always incorporated heart and feeling into our governance and decision-making. In colonial systems feelings and emotions are often treated as weaknesses in leadership, and over time we've been taught to ignore our feelings and doubt ourselves. This disconnect makes it difficult for us to trust what we know and how we feel. But our ways teach us that feeling is essential to knowing, that our hearts and minds should work together.

The work we are doing to reclaim our lands, our rights, and our sovereignty, to decolonize and heal, has never been done before. There is no map for this journey; we are creating it as we go. This requires the courage to move forward, to explore uncharted paths. Everything we learn along the way will lay down a foundation for those coming after us. This work isn't just about survival, it's about creating a healthy future for our children built on trust in ourselves, each other, and the wisdom we carry.

Colonial systems lead from the head, rooted in a need for control and predictability, pushing us to believe that, without a fully laid-out path, we're not ready to start. In this way of thinking we're expected to piece together every possible outcome, every solution, before we even take a step forward. This mindset doesn't leave room for trust or intuition, it assumes that uncertainty is a failure, that every answer has to be found in advance.

In our teachings, it's different. Our elders tell us that understanding comes through doing, through being present in the experience itself. They remind us that you can't fully know something until you engage with it—not by standing on the sidelines but by moving through it with an open heart. We're told, "You don't have to know everything before you start. Just take that first step. Trust that you will understand as you go."

But it's hard for many people to embrace this. After generations of being taught to doubt our feelings, we hesitate to follow our instincts. Colonial systems have conditioned us to see action without complete certainty of the result as reckless. We've learned to mistrust the idea of "just doing" because it feels vulnerable, as though we're walking into something without armour. We question ourselves: "What if I make a mistake? What if I don't have all the answers?"

Our teachings, however, hold a different kind of wisdom. They tell us that real understanding, the kind that stays with you, is born from experience, not from overthinking every detail. When we move with intention but without the need for total control, we find that the knowledge we seek is waiting for us along the way. But to reach it we have to let go of the need to predict every outcome, and instead trust in our own ability to adapt, to learn, to grow as we go.

It's a radical shift from the safety and control of colonial thinking. It's about having the courage to lean into the unknown and trust that we will find our way through it. In the end our teachings ask us not to pre-plan each step, but to let each one reveal the path forward.

It's important to understand that our traditions are not based on a single, uniform set of practices for everyone in a community or family, much less an entire nation. In times past each family had its own ways, roles, and responsibilities to the community and the land. Individuals had specific roles within their families, and each person knew their strengths and areas where they could contribute. They didn't need to be told, and they didn't wait for permission to be who they were.

Colonization disrupted this understanding. It taught us to rely on external authorities—teachers, parents, bosses—to tell us what to do and how to do it. We became accustomed to being graded, promoted, demoted, or even shamed if we didn't perform in a prescribed way.

In our earlier communities, we didn't need to be graded or told what to do. We were raised with the confidence that we had something unique to contribute to our family, community, and nation. Instead of asking, "What can they do for me?" or "What will I get?" we understood our responsibility to contribute to the well-being of everyone around us.

This understanding is what coming-of-age practices instill. They teach us confidence and help us remember who we are. These teachings remind us that we were born good and that we belong here. Today's systems, however, often make us feel like we're not enough, like we don't belong or aren't capable. That mindset creates fear and insecurity, which are poor foundations for making good decisions.

These traditional teachings are important for everyone because they help us find our sense of self-worth, purpose, and connection, qualities that allow us to make decisions with confidence rather than fear.

There are countless practices from around the world that guide people in spirituality, self-love, and self-confidence. These ways are neither right nor wrong, they simply are. They reflect the values and wisdom of the cultures that created them. What works for one person might not resonate with another, and that's okay. Each teaching and practice offer a different pathway, a unique perspective, and how you interpret these teachings is yours to discover and understand.

It's about finding what feels true for you, without judgment. It's not about being right or wrong, but about exploring ways of being that bring you closer to yourself.

Coming-of-age ceremonies start from the moment you are born. In my family, the grandparents are present in the birthing room and the first to speak to our babies, who are welcomed with songs and brushed off. "Brushing off" is a traditional practice wherein we use an eagle feather to sweep away anything that doesn't serve the person, like negative energy or burdens that are clinging to them. It's more than just removing what's heavy, it's also about brushing medicine onto them, filling that space with something positive, healing, and protective. The feather helps the child to become grounded and renewed, carrying only what truly belongs to them.

The first words our babies hear are ones of love and affirmation. They are given names as soon as they are born. They are told that they are special, that we were waiting for them to come. They are told who they are, who their family is, and what nation they have been born into. They are told of the land they belong to.

Our children are given a sense of identity the moment they come into the world. When they fall off, our babies' belly buttons are buried by a tree or sweat lodge in their territory. This is so the baby will grow up feeling a connection to a land and know they belong there.

Indigenous Peoples have always upheld our children for their sacredness. We believe that children are chosen by their parents before they come to earth, arriving with a purpose and a connection to the spirit world. They are seen as close to the Creator, able to travel back and forth between our world and the spirit world until the soft spot on their heads closes. This sacred connection is why they are revered and treated with such care—because they carry wisdom, innocence, and a closeness to the Creator that reminds us of who we are.

The elders in my family always told me that everything was done for good reason. We didn't just do things for the heck of it, there was purpose that contributed to the overall good of the family and community. We understood the way the world worked by observing the land and listening to our stories. Our people were scientists, doctors, and artists.

We understand trauma as a fact of life, something inescapable. When you are born into this world it's accepted that you will experience loss, pain, and suffering that impacts your whole being—your mind, body, and spirit—and influences how you show up in your community. Failing to care for yourself during these times can lead to chaos within, affecting everything around you: your family, your community, your nation, and even the land itself.

Part of our work is to ensure that everyone born into our communities is prepared for hard times. We prepare our bodies to endure the elements and the changing seasons. We know we cannot control the land and must adapt to it, so we expose ourselves to extreme heat and cold to help our bodies adjust and build resilience against the elements.

We also prepare our minds and spirits for grief and loss. Our people have a one-year protocol for families who lose a loved one. We understand that grieving makes people behave unlike themselves, making it easy to become sidetracked or trapped in memories, which can interfere with their ability to contribute. This means that when they are supposed to be gathering, fishing or hunting, they might become distracted and a liability.

When our family loses someone we are told to be still for one year to grieve fully. We have songs to help our families cry, and other families step up to provide food and necessities during that year. Sometimes, when we must bury people where they pass, we still follow certain protocols to honour the spirit and the family. A four-day ceremony supports the crossing over of the spirit, with the understanding that it takes that long for the spirit to visit all the places it touched during its lifetime to say goodbye.

During this period extended family members help the immediate family gather the belongings of the deceased to be burned, ensuring the spirit doesn't linger. We boil wild rose bushes to make a red water that cleanses the home or camp, removing lingering spirits or energies. The family also bathes in this water to prevent the spirit from clinging to them.

Our community gathers to sit with the family, cook and sing for them, and help care for the deceased relative. This time together helps ground the family in the present so they don't get lost in the past.

Five small strips of tanned buckskin are given to each grieving family member, indicating that they are in mourning. We are told to wear these ties as long as they remain intact, which may last from nine to eighteen months. Once the last tie falls off our period of grieving is considered complete.

Strips are tied around the neck, wrists, and ankles. These serve as reminders for ourselves and others that we are grieving, that healing takes time. The tie around our necks reminds us to be mindful of our words, the ties around our wrists remind us to be careful with our actions, and the ties around our ankles remind us to be thoughtful about where we walk during this time, as grief can make us act in ways that don't reflect our true selves.

Science now tells us that it takes the brain about a year to heal from grief. Research in psychology reveals that grieving changes the brain, disrupting memory, emotion, and decision-making. The limbic system, which processes emotions, is particularly affected, making it harder for people to regulate their feelings and react calmly. Grieving individuals often experience heightened stress responses, which can interfere with their ability to focus, make decisions, and engage in daily activities.

This scientific insight aligns with our traditional wisdom: we have always known that grief and loss are deeply traumatic, affecting how we think, feel, and behave in ways that others may not immediately understand.

Tears, too, play a vital role in this process. Studies indicate that crying is a natural mechanism for releasing stress hormones and rebalancing the brain's chemistry. It's as if our bodies and minds are equipped with their own ways of processing and healing from trauma, helping us release some of the pain and confusion that comes with grief. When we cry it's not just an emotional release, it's part of the body's effort to reset, allowing space for healing to begin.

In times of trauma we often struggle to function, create, or problem-solve. Grief and trauma have a way of narrowing our focus, leaving us stuck in cynicism and helplessness. In these times the only real way others can support us is by cultivating an environment of safety, connection, and belonging. These elements provide the foundation we need to slowly rebuild ourselves and rediscover our sense of purpose, as we process the deep emotions that come with loss.

When our children in the past were coming of age, they were introduced to the other families in the community so they would know who they were and which family they belonged to, and these families also become responsible for the safety and health of the child. The child would then know who else they could go to for help. This developed a sense of belonging, connection, and identity, which let them feel safe. When children feel safe and connected, they function to their highest potential. They can absorb and process information and problem-solve creatively.

The elders paid attention to the children, how they acted and moved and spoke. They noted their light and their gifts. They encouraged the children to master these gifts, which would strengthen the family and contribute to the community and nation.

All of this was important for the health of our systems. The introduction of colonialism stripped our communities of this health. It began by the removal of the children from our families, communities, nations, and lands. It stripped people of their identity and knowledge of who they were and where they came from. It disconnected us from our lands.

Colonialism robbed Indigenous Peoples of our identity and knowledge. It disconnected us from our lands so they could be stripped of their resources for money and power. It built a system of fear and control to keep our people hopeless. Colonialism even stripped the settlers coming to the Americas of who they were, and they too became disconnected from their lands, languages, and families.

Each family carries teachings and responsibilities to contribute to the overall health of the community and future generations. Today we are afraid to share what we know because we don't want to seem *different*. We keep our gifts and teachings to ourselves and our immediate families because of the fear of rejection, of the inability to trust ourselves and each other.

Our communities have been stripped of so much, but we still know who we are and where we come from: it lives in our blood and language and stories. Colonialism has conditioned us to believe we all have to do things and behave a certain way to belong and be successful. Colonialism has told us there is not enough for everyone, teaching us to make decisions out of fear of poverty.

Colonialism has made us believe that if people don't show up where we are, they don't care about the cause. It makes us think that to truly be Indigenous, we have to look a certain way, know certain things, and have been raised a certain way. We're expected to fit a narrow mould; wear traditional clothing, beadwork, and feathers; speak our language fluently, and have an intimate knowledge of all our cultural teachings. If we don't we're often judged, both by others and ourselves, as somehow less authentic.

Many Indigenous Peoples today didn't grow up with these experiences because of the effects of colonization and assimilation policies, which deliberately stripped away our languages, ceremonies, and traditional ways of life. Some of us were raised in urban settings away from our traditional territories, or in households where our teachings couldn't be openly practiced. Others were raised in foster care or adopted by non-Indigenous families, disconnected from our cultures. Colonialism has imposed these ideas on us, creating the false notion that we are only *real* if we match an idealized image of what Indigenous identity should be.

Our teachings never left us, we just forgot how to trust ourselves. Sometimes all we need to do is stop, reflect on the things we know, and see the patterns in how we make decisions. We don't know why we make them, it's just what we've always done. Sometimes we just have an instinct on how to respond, an idea or a gut feeling, but we hold back because we've become good at silencing the ancestral knowledge that has been passed onto us without us even knowing.

As you reach the end of this chapter, take a moment to reflect on what coming-of-age truly means—not as a simple passage of time, but as a profound reconnection to who we are and where we come from. Our ancestors knew that identity is shaped through the experiences we share with our families, communities, and the land. The journey to self-discovery and resilience isn't something we can learn in isolation; it requires us to listen, feel, and engage deeply with the world around us.

Elders teach that coming-of-age ceremonies are essential to healing trauma and reducing violence because they reconnect us to our identity, community, and purpose. In our traditions coming-of-age goes beyond reaching a certain age, it's a path to knowing ourselves, discovering our gifts, and understanding our responsibilities to our families, our communities, and the land. Through these practices, we root ourselves in belonging, confidence, and self-worth, qualities that shield us from the cycles of fear and disconnection that often lead to trauma and harm.

By embracing these traditions we build resilience and cultivate a sense of safety, mutual respect, and grounded identity. When we understand our place in the world and feel valued for who we are, we're less likely to seek power through control or violence. Instead, we approach challenges with empathy, cooperation, and courage. This is the power of self-determination, knowing who we are and where we come from, a vision of healing that extends out to strengthen our entire community.

Ask yourself how you connect to the teachings, stories, and practices of your own lineage. What lessons from your past or family history bring you strength and purpose? In a world that often pressures us to conform, how can you honour your unique path and gifts? And as you reflect on what it means to come of age in your own life, what steps can you take to root yourself more fully in who you are and the community you belong to?

Let these questions guide you back to your roots, grounding yourself in the knowledge that you are part of something larger, something that carries the strength and resilience of all those who came before you.

Chapter 7

MODERN MENTORSHIP

I have always known that in every book I write, I will acknowledge the many people who have contributed to my journey, just as I did in my first book, *Calling My Spirit Back*. I never preplan who I'll talk about; the names come to me as I write. I am committed to finding ways to honour and recognize those who have mentored me, who have shared their knowledge and kindness. This is what I was taught: you always share what you know and acknowledge those who helped shape you. I am community-grown. I am a reflection of all the people, all the families, who have held me, taught me, and walked with me along the way. This chapter is part of that commitment, a way to honour Greg and all the mentors who have shown me what it means to listen, hold space, and lead with quiet strength.

Greg has been one of those mentors, a steady presence who guided me through some of the hardest moments in my life. Reflecting on the role he's played in my journey, I see that his mentorship has been about more than just advice. It's been a model for how to hold space for others, to listen with patience, and to lead with quiet strength. This kind of mentorship has been crucial as I navigate this new phase of my life, not providing answers but helping me find them within myself, showing me the path forward without taking away my ability to choose my own way.

Coming of Age

Mentorship in our community isn't a formal process. It's woven into everyday life, in the quiet acts of support, unspoken understanding, and willingness to be there for one another even when words aren't enough. Through Greg and others I've come to understand that mentorship is an ongoing journey, growing and evolving with each coming-of-age moment in our lives. It's a gift that helps us navigate those pivotal transitions, reminding us that we're never alone on this path.

I hope that sharing these stories will help you recognize the mentors in your own life, the people who quietly guide and support you through the twists and turns. Mentorship isn't just about wisdom or advice, it's about walking with someone through life's challenges, offering strength when they falter, and helping them find their own way forward.

It wasn't until I was in my thirties that I realized how much love and mentorship had been put into me since childhood. I've felt alone many times in my life. I believed that no one understood me and that everyone was against me. So many of us feel like that without seeing the mentors who have been there for us, helping us move through coming-of-age practices without realizing they were being done.

Some of my first happy memories with my mom were from when she worked at the band office on the reserve. When I was little our community was small compared to what it is today. Our main spaces were close together: the community hall and baseball diamond were just a few steps up the road from a community grave site, along with the heritage building, a playground, a church, and the band office. Around those main buildings were the homes of our oldest members. It was easy for young people and children to visit all of them.

My tema and mom always went visiting, and I would go with them. When I was a little older I would go into their homes on my own, where they would feed me or let me get a cup of water. I played with whatever kids were around. If we got in trouble, we were punished according to the rules of that home. If the home disciplined by spanking, then everyone was lined up and spanked, even if you weren't one of their kids. When trouble popped up, most of the time I knew it was my cue to run back to my tema's house. It wasn't called *abuse*, and if someone spanked another's kids no one got in trouble. No one called social services, no parents picked fights with the others. It was understood that it was everyone's responsibility to take care of the children.

The band office is where our programs and services are run from. Back when our band office was started my mom was the secretary, but by the time I was a kid she was working in the lands department, which manages and protects reserve lands and oversees land use, environmental stewardship, community development, and other services like land transfers, wills, and estates to uphold the community's cultural values and rights.

The lands department was more than a job for her, it was a role that allowed her to live her values and serve our community in a way that resonated deeply with who she was. She was passionate about politics and governance, driven by an unwavering commitment to Indigenous rights and our responsibilities as syilx people. Though she wasn't an elected leader, her work in the lands department allowed her to protect our community's land, culture, and future while advocating for self-determination and autonomy.

She carried a clear understanding of title and rights. She saw her work as an extension of our community's broader struggle for justice. She didn't just see herself as an employee, but as a protector of our land and culture, ensuring that every action taken in the department honoured our people's connection to the land.

But what truly set her apart was her ability to connect with people. My mom had a rare gift: she got along with everyone, regardless of family ties or community divisions. She held genuine relationships with all the families in our community, a quality that allowed her to approach sensitive matters with care and understanding. When it came to complex issues like wills, estates, and land transfers, she could bridge gaps between families, handling each case with the compassion and respect it deserved. These were often emotionally charged discussions, tied to family legacies and our shared identity as syilx people, and her relationships allowed her to navigate these moments with grace.

Through her work my mom embodied the values she believed in: responsibility, care, resilience, and connection. She knew that her role wasn't just about managing land, it was about protecting our community's future while honouring the bonds between families and the responsibilities we hold to one another. She built trust in her relationships, blending her radical commitment to Indigenous rights with a warmth and openness that made her a bridge within the community. Her presence in the lands department allowed her to support community members in ways that went far beyond the official scope of her work.

As the band office expanded to meet the growing needs of our people, it became more than just an administrative hub. It grew to a place where our community's heart and needs converged. A few staff members worked in social development, providing critical services that ranged from social assistance to education programs, and my mom's role in the lands department made her a key part of that network of support. For Evelyn and me, the office became a second home. Our school bus had a main stop right in front, and we would often get off there after school to meet our mom.

As soon as we entered the building we would head straight for our band manager Greg Gabriel's office. As soon as we walked in a big smile would break out across his face. He would welcome us into his space and ask us what we were doing there, chuckling because he knew we were there for the stash of gum he always kept in his desk drawer.

For many communities the roles of chief, council member, and band manager are among the hardest positions to hold. They are often targets for hurt, mistrust, and anger, and it's rare that anyone is truly satisfied with the people in those roles. What many of our community members didn't realize, though, is that these positions come with constraints imposed by the Indian Act, leaving our leaders with limited decision-making power within the narrow box of rules forced upon us. The Indian Act was built to turn us against each other, making it all the more challenging for those in leadership to build the trust and connection that my mom and Greg managed to foster every day.

As a little girl I was always amazed at how Greg was so welcoming to people who came to him. His door was always open. Sometimes he would get a serious look on his face when someone came to him, and quietly welcome them into his space. Sometimes people would happily walk into his office to update him on how things were progressing, laughing and joking, and other times they would be mad and yelling, but I never saw him lose his cool.

He was always quiet at community meetings, listening to everyone share, and when people were upset he would simply sit and listen. When it was his turn to talk he always had a steady and confident voice, and a plan. He paid attention to what people wanted and he was always able to come up with some kind of solution on how to move forward to address all the issues and concerns people raised.

When I got older my first job was as the education assistant at the band office on a summer job placement. Greg was someone I could go to easily. Whenever I was asked to bring paperwork to him, he would say, "Well, what do you need?" I'd add the papers to the piles already on his desk and he would read over them, maybe ask a question, and then sign them for me to bring back to my manager.

He was someone I learned I could be open with, and when I struggled with a problem I could always go to him. Whenever I was conflicted, upset over how to deal with boundaries or conflict, he never let my emotions distract him from what was really going on. When I asked for time off to go to a powwow, he would tell me it was awesome I wanted to participate. This was before Indigenous organizations started giving people time off for cultural activities. When I became pregnant with my son at seventeen he congratulated me, and I was welcomed back to work with open arms after Kyle was born.

In 1996 my mom had a massive stroke that left her unable to speak. I was nineteen. She had two major aneurysms in her brain, and she had to undergo massive surgery. I knew my mom confided in Greg, as did many of our community members. He honoured so many of those disclosures, and I acknowledge how difficult it can be to hold the stories of so many people from your own community.

Greg was a witness to my mom's will—she wrote it when she got sick. I didn't know this until after she had passed away. What a burden he must have carried to know my mom was sick, and to honour her request to protect me and Evelyn, only nineteen and seventeen at the time.

Without even knowing this he was the first person I called when I found out my mom had a major stroke. I was on my way home to be with her in the hospital when I got stuck in a blizzard. I had no money, no credit card, and just enough gas to make it home. I was on a payphone in the lobby of a roadside motel in Abbotsford, letting him know I didn't know what to do, that there was no place to go, and I might have to find a church or community hall to sleep in.

The front desk staff heard me. They called out to let me know they just received a cancellation and would give me a room, but I told them I didn't have any money. Greg told me to give him the front desk's phone number. He called and filled out a preauthorization form for me to stay in the room, so I didn't get stuck on the side of the highway like so many other stranded travellers.

It was hard for me after mom had her stroke. Even though she was still with us, she couldn't speak or guide me anymore. But so many people from my community stepped up to support Evelyn and me. I did my best to manage my mom's affairs at the age of nineteen, her debt and paperwork and bills. We brought her home after she was released from the hospital and Evelyn and I had to care for her.

This was when the families in our community stepped up to support us. Each played instrumental roles in helping raise us into adulthood, because she was a single mom and we never had a real father figure in our life. It was a difficult time because I had split with my son's dad, and I didn't know anything about money. Within six months of my mom's stroke, I started to drink again and spiralled out of control. (I go into detail about this journey and much more in my previous book, *Calling My Spirit Back*.)

Mentorship of our young people isn't the way it once was, a natural, everyday responsibility that everyone took on as part of community life. In the past mentorship wasn't something we thought of as "formal" or "structured," it was just a way of being, a shared understanding that everyone held a role in guiding and supporting each other. We valued each person's growth and well-being and the whole community took part in helping each individual find their place and purpose. This wasn't an extra task or something set apart, it was woven into everything we did.

Now, as the pressures of modern life and the impacts of colonialism have influenced our communities, mentorship can feel more like a separate, intentional act. Taking time for coming-of-age guidance and mentorship sometimes feels formalized, something we consciously carve out rather than letting it flow naturally through daily life. But in truth, our way of mentoring never really disappeared. It's in our blood. This tradition of mentorship is something we carry on without even realizing it—it just happens, organically and instinctively. When I was angry, lost in my grief, and struggling to ask for help, I thought people had given up on me. But when I was finally ready to do the internal work I saw that so many of them had been there all along, quietly supporting me in ways I didn't fully see at the time.

Continuing meaningful mentorship comes with many challenges in our community. Many of our families live below the poverty line, dealing with both unresolved trauma and a lack of basic resources. How are we supposed to mentor and support each other when so many of us are barely making it ourselves? We struggle not only to meet basic needs like food, housing, and healthcare, but we face stereotypes and systemic racism that affect how we see ourselves and each other. These layered barriers make it hard for us to lift each other up when we're fighting to simply survive.

Only recently have I fully understood the harm colonial systems have inflicted on our people, particularly through education. Colonial teachings made us question everything about ourselves. As a child I was taught to feel stupid, to feel *less than*, a message ingrained in me from a young age. Our reserves are funded by the federal government, and this often reflects the lowest possible standards. Housing and infrastructure contracts must be approved through government processes, which usually mean accepting the lowest bids. As a result the quality of work and resources we receive is poor, and we've come to expect the bare minimum. It's as if we've been conditioned to believe this is all we deserve.

Generations of this treatment have taught us to settle for what we're given. When we're continually told by our education system that we aren't good enough or smart enough, our confidence and sense of self-worth erodes. Racism isn't just something we encounter in the outside world, it's embedded in the systems that govern us, influencing everything from our access to resources to our internal sense of safety.

When we don't feel safe, valued, or confident, it becomes difficult to show up fully for others. Sometimes, in our hurt and frustration, we turn that pain inward, or we take it out on those around us. It's hard to build trust with others when we've been taught not to trust ourselves. The systemic forces that work against us don't just impact individuals, they affect the very fabric of our communities, making it harder to create the conditions for mentorship, guidance, and collective healing.

The leaders in our community who have been raised by our matriarchs carry the teachings they've inherited in everything they do. I see it in the way they share, hold space, listen, and trust, especially in moments when others don't extend that trust to them. Our communities are full of mistrust, and the weight of this can make leadership even more challenging. But those who carry the matriarchs' teachings continue to show up with resilience and integrity, choosing to trust and believe in people despite the risks.

I remember a time when Greg called me into his office because he wanted to know why Evelyn was helping me on a project and being paid $500. I explained that I had put out a call in the community newsletter for assistance but no one had responded, so Evelyn stepped in to help.

There was an added layer of complexity here because Evelyn was family, and in our community nepotism is a sensitive topic. Some people perceive any family connection in work as favoritism, especially when funding is involved. Greg needed to understand the details so he could support my decision if questions or complaints came up. He wanted to be ready to stand behind the work with a clear understanding of my reasoning.

Issues of nepotism in community run deep, and I've experienced this firsthand. Because of my past there were people who didn't want to support me, either because they didn't like me or because they judged me for my struggles. I was constantly dealing with my alcoholism and making questionable choices, and that reputation followed me. Some people saw me as a risk, not worth the effort or trust.

When I needed help I found that often the only people who stepped up were my close family and friends, and many times they helped me simply out of love, even when there was no payment involved. They were there for me when others weren't, showing up to support me in ways that I couldn't always find outside my close circles.

Greg's support meant a lot, but back then I would often feel defensive or scared, convinced that people didn't like me or the work I was doing. I always had a protective wall up, fearful of being attacked or rejected. One day Greg asked me why I felt that way, and all I could say was, "I don't know." He looked at me with calm reassurance and said, "You know, no one has ever come into my office and said that you're bad at what you do. Not one person has ever complained about your work. You're doing all right."

Hearing that made me break down in tears, but I felt safe crying in his office. He had built a space where I could be vulnerable, where I didn't have to hide my insecurities or doubts. He wanted me to feel confident, to see my own potential, and to be courageous. He always told me he was proud of me, and if I ever did something questionable he would address it directly, with honesty and kindness.

Greg modelled the importance of following processes, understanding procedures, and respecting policies, of being as fair as possible in decisions. He taught me to know when to slow down and reflect and when to take decisive action. He invited me into meetings, not just as an observer but as a participant, encouraging me to listen, learn, and present. He showed me the value of knowing who I was speaking to, when to be thorough and detailed, and when it was best to be brief and to the point. Greg taught me to speak fast when necessary and, most importantly, to speak up.

Through his mentorship I learned not just about the technicalities of leadership, but about leading with trust, compassion, and a willingness to believe in others even when they struggled to believe in themselves. Greg helped me peel back the layers of fear that held me back, allowing me to see myself through his eyes as a person worthy of trust, confidence, and respect. There were few people in my community who made me feel that way.

When I went to Greg in his role of band manager, he had a way of making me feel seen and valued. He did his best to show up for everyone, even those who might be frustrated or upset with him. He knew how to navigate those tensions with empathy. No matter the time of day Greg would show up when people needed him, even if there had been conflict between them. Often it was community members who felt unheard or overlooked, and Greg had the ability to listen and support them, even after a tense interaction. He always followed up with someone to make sure issues brought to his attention were addressed.

But Greg was also a person of action. When a crisis came up, he didn't hesitate. He understood that there are times to hold space and listen and times to take charge and do what needs to be done. He would assess emergency situations quickly and respond with calm determination, guiding others with clarity and purpose. Greg's leadership was about balancing the care for his people with the courage to act. He taught me that leadership is both heart and hands, showing up for people and taking action when it counts.

One day Evelyn and I were at home when a black bear appeared outside our sliding glass door. It was huge, lingering in a way that made us nervous, as though it was bold enough to try to come inside. We yelled to scare it off, but it didn't move. Finally we called Greg. It was late, but he just said, "All right, I'm on my way."

Greg lived a few minutes away, and within moments he pulled up in his truck, high beams on and horn blaring. He drove right up to the bear and chased it off. He jumped out, looked around, and focused on our garbage can, its contents spilling onto the ground. He picked up the garbage, put the lid on, and moved the bin to the end of the driveway. As he walked back, he told us we needed to be more careful with our trash. This was just one example of the countless times he showed up for me and my family, offering help in the way only he could.

As a teenager I didn't always appreciate him. I was going through my wild phase, drinking a lot and throwing parties, and

Greg was often the one telling me to stop, especially when it was at my mom's house. He was the kind of mentor who tells you things you might not want to hear, but you need to in order to grow. At the time I didn't like it, but looking back I see how valuable his guidance was. His patience and honesty taught me lessons that resonate in my life today.

The common thread between Greg and the other mentors in my life is trust. Greg trusted people to do good work. He didn't need to know every detail, he trusted that it would get done. When people came to him, even when they were angry and yelling—which was often the case with frustrated community members—he would listen without reacting, finding out what they truly needed. He understood that trust and patience were foundational to leadership.

Not all my mentors have been around for long periods, but each one taught me something important. Some of them challenged me, and I didn't always agree with their approach, but I was taught to listen for the lesson, to take what I needed and leave the rest. That openness to learning has helped me understand people and cultivate empathy.

It takes a special kind of leader to listen calmly when people are angry and not react. This practice of patient listening is something our elders have modelled, a quality essential for cultivating safe spaces. We often overlook those in our community who quietly carry forward our traditional ways. Greg would mention how he valued our language and culture, though I sensed that he felt a distance from it, perhaps because he didn't speak the language himself. I watched how people interacted with him, sometimes questioning his connection to our traditions.

Yet despite that perceived distance, Greg embodied the spirit of our teachings in everything he did. His patience, discipline, and way of listening were rooted in the ancient values he'd absorbed, especially from his mother, Louise Gabriel, the respected elder and trailblazer mentioned earlier.

Louise's influence was clear in Greg's actions. Even if he didn't speak the language, he carried those teachings in the way he led and held space for others. His approach reflected the wisdom and strength of our elders, a legacy of resilience and respect. He might not have claimed to be deeply connected to every tradition but his spirit and leadership showed otherwise. Through him I saw how traditional teachings could live on quietly, shaping us not by words but by the way we show up for each other.

Reflecting on Greg's impact, I see how his mentorship helped me come of age in ways I didn't understand at the time. Modern mentorship may look different, but the heart of it remains the same: showing up, offering guidance, and holding space for growth. Greg taught me that mentorship doesn't always come in the form of formal lessons or structured advice. Sometimes it's in the steady presence, the quiet acts of support, and the willingness to tell you what you need to hear, even when it's hard.

As I navigate my own journey I realize that I carry those same teachings, passed from Greg, who learned them from Louise, who inherited them from our ancestors. This is the legacy of mentorship in our community: an unbroken chain of guidance, resilience, and love woven through generations. I see now that coming of age is not a single event but a continuous process, one that calls us to learn, grow, and carry forward the wisdom of those who came before us. In honouring their teachings we honour ourselves, and we prepare to guide those who will come after us.

Take a moment to think about the mentors who have quietly shaped your life. Who are the people who have offered you guidance, perhaps without you even noticing it at the time? They might have shown up for you in small but significant ways, modelling resilience, trust, or compassion. Consider what they taught you and how those lessons continue to shape who you are today.

How might you carry forward those teachings in your own life, in the way you show up for others? Mentorship can be as simple as listening, as profound as trusting others to find their path, or as brave as speaking hard truths with kindness. Think about the legacy you want to pass on and remember that coming-of-age and becoming a mentor are journeys we're all on together.

Chapter 8

FOUR FOOD CHIEFS

Before people came to be, there were animal people who roamed the earth. One day, the Creator came down and said to the Four Food Chiefs, "There is going to be a new being that walks this earth, and I want you to figure out how this being will survive." Then he put the being between the chiefs and left.

The Four Food Chiefs are skemxist, Chief Black Bear, who was chief of the four-legged and winged animals; siya, Chief Saskatoon Berry, who was chief of all the plants that grew above ground; spitlem, Chief Bitterroot, who was chief of all the plants that grew below ground; and n'tytiyixw, Chief Spring Salmon, who was chief of all the animals in the water.

The chiefs all looked at the being that was left in the centre and said, "This is the most pitiful being I have ever seen. How is it supposed to survive? It has an empty head, no fur to keep it warm, and no teeth to help it eat. It can't even run away if it needs to."

The chiefs looked to Chief Black Bear, who was the eldest, and said, "You're the oldest, you tell us what you're going to do." Chief Black Bear thought about it and thought about it. Finally he said, "I will lay down my life for this being, and it can use my body for whatever it needs to survive."

The other chiefs looked at each other and said that they too would give up their lives for this being. So Chief Black Bear laid his body on the ground and told the others, "I will lay my life down now and it is up to you to sing me back to life."

Chief Black Bear laid down and the chiefs gathered around to sing their songs to bring him back to life. The chiefs finished their songs, but Chief Black Bear didn't come back to life. All of the other animals and plants and fish and winged ones came to sing their songs, but still Chief Black Bear didn't come back to life.

As all of the animal people stood around Chief Black Bear, Fly came buzzing around, trying to get past everyone, saying, "Please, let me sing my song. I want to sing my song." All of the animal people swatted Fly away, saying, "Go away, no one wants to hear your song. All you do is bug people and eat crap. Go away." But Fly managed to get through the people and sit on Chief Black Bear's ear, and there he sang his song.

Chief Black Bear rose and came back to life.

This story is told from my memory, and I have heard a variation of it by different people from different families or parts of the nation. Each storyteller emphasizes a different teaching, and every time I hear someone else tell it I learn something new.

When I hear the story I think about how our thoughts and ideas are important in all spaces, even if the thought seems meaningless and insignificant. It also shares that we need to make space and listen to even the annoying ones, the ones we don't like, the ones we tend to leave out.

Our language and stories and structures tell us that it is important to know who we are, where we come from, where we belong to, and to be confident in what we know and what wisdom we were born with, even if it doesn't make sense to anyone else. It is important for us to listen and hear each other's voices and bring them together in way that moves us forward together.

Our people share this story as part of our decision-making and governance systems. It is the ultimate reminder that we are part of all living things, and it is important for us to remember to honour them, to share songs, and to listen to all voices, even the ones we find annoying. We are taught that when we use all parts of the animal and don't leave anything for waste, we can regenerate life.

We are taught that when we have the patience to listen to all the voices, we are so powerful that we can bring back life. This story also talks about the importance of including different voices, even the ones we don't understand. A big part of including voices is listening to them even when we don't agree with what they are saying.

Many of us were taught to doubt ourselves from the moment we came into this world. We were taught that anything different isn't good, and when we think differently we are made fun of and told we are stupid, that we don't make sense, that we need to get on the same page as everyone else. We learn to become small and do things to fit in, because it hurts to feel excluded and left behind.

When we are asked to practice our self-determination we hesitate and wait for someone else, because we do not want to make mistakes. We do not want to be told we are wrong, and we wait for the rules to tell us how to think.

I had a conversation about this with my friend Charlie. He has a term for this imaginary revelation: the "messiah moment." When a group of people wanting to make radical change are asked how they're going to do this and they're not quite sure how to answer, they are hoping that a messiah moment will occur: someone will step in and tell them how to do it. We are all guilty of this at one time or another, just waiting for someone to tell us what to do because we are scared to make a mistake and do it wrong.

Colonial systems are completely fear-driven and based on control. Policies are written by people in places of privilege and intended to support a structure, business, or system, not a people. Community members are forced to make decisions under an immense amount of pressure. We tend to make issues about *people*, not the system. These systems are built to make us doubt ourselves.

When I attend political meetings I often see leadership attacking each other, asking, "Why aren't you doing enough?" or, "You're doing it wrong!" They instill fear and doubt in each other. *You're working too slow. You're moving too fast.*

When leadership returns home to their communities they often face criticism from their own people: "Why aren't you doing enough? You're doing it wrong!" This frustration arises because so many of us feel powerless. We struggle, live in poverty, see injustice, and experience suffering all around us. Sometimes, in our attempts to reclaim a sense of power, we turn on each other, making others feel small as a way of soothing our own pain. This anger stems from a perception that others haven't acted quickly enough, or that they made mistakes, or simply didn't do things "right." For those in leadership and staff positions this creates a cycle of fear. They begin to doubt themselves, stay in safe zones, and conform to systems just to avoid criticism. This pressure can lead them to rely on colonial systems as a form of protection and control rather than innovating or trusting their instincts. One such system is "Robert's Rules of Order," established by Henry Robert, a U.S. Army officer in San Francisco in 1876. This rulebook is still widely used to structure meetings, permitting only certain people to speak at designated times. It fosters exclusion, control, and rigidity, suppressing the very ideas and emotions that might lead to true progress. In these highly controlled spaces people don't feel safe or connected, which stifles creativity and innovation.

Self-determination, however, is about trusting ourselves and encouraging a space where everyone's voice matters. It's about listening openly even when we disagree or don't fully understand each other. This practice unites thoughts and solutions, nurturing belonging, freedom, and wellbeing for all. Practicing self-determination also means working from our strengths and recognizing that none of us has all the answers, but together we can find them. It's essential to talk to each other, hear each other's stories, and make space for ideas, even those that seem unconventional or out of reach. Sometimes the missing voice or song is what holds the key.

The story of the Four Food Chiefs helps me reflect on the importance of self-determination and balance in how I show up in spaces where decisions are made. Each chief in the story demonstrated sacrifice, responsibility, and the willingness to give of themselves to sustain the people who would come after them. No one told them what to do; each chief chose to offer their gifts in their own way, without external pressure or instructions. This story is a reminder of the strength that comes from within, from knowing who we are and what we can offer, and from trusting that each of us has something valuable to contribute.

When I show up in meetings I hold myself accountable to those teachings. I don't need anyone to tell me how to act or what my role should be. True self-determination means that I am responsible for keeping myself in line: showing up with integrity, listening to others, and being mindful of the impact of my words and actions. It's not about following someone else's rules, it's about following the values and principles that have been passed down to me. This approach allows me to participate fully and authentically, knowing that I bring my unique song to the circle.

But to sustain this way of being I also have to care for myself. The Four Food Chiefs story teaches that giving of oneself should be balanced with restoration. Just as they gave their lives to feed the new beings, we too must nurture and replenish ourselves if we want to contribute meaningfully over the long term. For me this means being intentional about how I put back what I take, whether that's restoring my energy after giving to others or caring for the land that sustains us.

In the end the way we care for ourselves reflects in how we care for our communities and the land. The story reminds us that when we lead from a place of balance and respect, honouring our own needs alongside those of others, we create the conditions for a healthier future. We show up grounded, guided by our values, ready to listen and act with purpose. This is the path of true self-determination, where we govern ourselves not through control or fear, but through respect, trust, and connection.

In many Western contexts, self-care is often viewed as something individualistic, like indulgence, which is sometimes dismissed as "navel-gazing." This kind of self-care can become twisted into an excuse to shut out the world, focusing inward without regard for how one's well-being connects to others. But our understanding of self-care is different. For us, taking care of ourselves is essential but it is not about retreating from our responsibilities. Instead it's about showing up better for our communities and honouring the responsibilities we hold.

Our people understood that taking care of ourselves is a necessary foundation for contributing to the greater well-being of everyone around us. If we are burned out, lost in our own sadness, or overwhelmed by anger, it affects how we show up in decision-making and how we uphold our duties to all living things. Self-care, in our teachings, isn't about placing ourselves above others or isolating ourselves from the community. It's about building the strength to return to the circle with clarity, balance, and purpose.

Part of coming-of-age, especially in our decision-making processes, is learning how to regulate ourselves so that we can approach decisions from the highest parts of ourselves, not from reactive places in our minds that breed cynicism and judgment. This kind of self-regulation is crucial because it allows us to listen openly, without bias clouding our perception. When we are centred and grounded we can hold space for different ideas and come up with solutions that foster coexistence with all living things.

In governance these stories become our compass. They remind us of what it means to truly take responsibility for ourselves and each other. Through telling stories like the Four Food Chiefs before every meeting, we remind ourselves that leadership is not about control but balance, respect, and interdependence. The chiefs' willingness to sacrifice for the survival of a helpless being shows us a path to inclusive decision-making and compassion in action, one that serves as a model for all forms of governance, from family circles to entire nations.

Ultimately the way we care for ourselves is woven into how we care for our communities and the land. The Four Food Chiefs remind us that balanced, respectful leadership, one that honours our needs as well as the needs of those around us, lays the foundation for a healthier, more connected future. This is true self-determination: a path where we govern ourselves with respect, trust, and interdependence rather than isolation or a narrow view of self-care.

How might you approach your leadership or decision-making differently if you were guided by the principles of respect, sacrifice, and collective responsibility that the Four Food Chiefs embody?

Think about a decision you're facing now. How would it change if you viewed it through the lens of not just what's best for you, but for the whole community or future generations? What part of yourself are you willing to lay down or let go of to serve a greater good, and what wisdom do you need to bring forward?

In embracing these teachings you might find that leadership is not just about getting things done, but about creating space for all voices, even the smallest ones, and acting in a way that uplifts and connects. What can you learn from others around you, even those you might usually overlook, and how might their "song" add something vital to your journey?

Chapter 9

SPIRIT HELPER

When I was a little girl, everyone would tell me how smart I was. Whenever I did something for an elder, talked to them or translated for them, they would get a proud look on their face, their eyes would go wide, and they would talk happily to my tema about my understanding. I felt special, especially when elders would take the time to share stories or teachings with me. Sometimes they scolded me or taught me in abrupt ways, but I learned much in those moments as well.

I had many elders and mentors who made me who I am. Each of them contributed to how I now show up in spaces and build up my confidence. They never asked for anything back, only that I share and take time to pay it forward. My tema was my primary teacher and I loved and trusted her with everything I was.

When my tema asked me to do something I trusted there was a reason behind it, even if I didn't fully understand it. She rarely explained and I learned not to question it—not because I wasn't allowed to but because some teachings are so layered they don't fit neatly into words, especially in English. In nsyilxcen a single word can carry multiple layers of meaning, holding a depth and complexity that doesn't easily translate. To fully explain one of these teachings would take a long time, unravelling connections and stories that go far beyond the words themselves.

Instead, the understanding was simply to "just do." By doing I would learn. I might not know or understand right away, but in time the experience would reveal its meaning when I needed it most. My tema's guidance was less about giving answers and more about guiding me to find them within myself. It was her way of teaching me that some knowledge only comes when we are ready, through living and trusting the journey.

When people in my community interact with each other and approach complicated issues, I see their teachings rise within them. It's in the patience they show each other when things get tough, in the way they act decisively when others might freeze, and in the unspoken coordination that emerges during times of need.

I see it especially during funerals, where each family instinctively contributes according to the teachings they've received. Some cook, others prepare headstones or gather fir boughs as medicine, or they support the grieving family by burning and letting go of items to help ensure the spirit doesn't hang on to the family. Some make sure the ground is ready for the gravesite, tending to every detail, spiritually and physically, while others light and watch over the sacred fire to keep it steady and undisturbed. Each person knows how to ready the land, to prepare themselves, and to support one another. They share their teachings openly, listen with respect until it's their turn then speak thoughtfully, informed by all they've heard.

In times of emergency I see this same instinctive coordination come alive. Roles are taken up without direction. Someone steps forward to organize, another handles communication, others move immediately into action to ensure preparation and safety. There are those who check on others, offer rides, gather supplies, and make sure everyone has what they need.

No one has to be told what to do; they feel the weight of their part in the whole and respond accordingly. This is how our teachings come through, quietly and naturally, each person stepping forward to contribute in the way they've been taught, grounded in a deep sense of belonging and responsibility.

At these gatherings elders would watch the younger ones closely, observing how each child responded in different situations—who knew how to listen, who was quick to act, who was inclined to play. And among those they would note who took risks and who held back. They noticed who moved quickly, who spoke up, who carried more emotion, and who naturally helped others. Through these quiet observations they recognized the unique strengths and qualities each child would bring to the community. They nurtured our gifts by seeing who we were and helping us understand our place within the larger whole.

Our families still carry the teachings of our ancestors, even if those lessons weren't passed down formally. Our elders didn't sit us down and say, *This is an Indian teaching; follow these ten steps and measure your success like this.* Instead the teachings came through lived experience, in ways that don't fit into simple instructions. Many of our older people still use the word "Indian" to refer to ourselves—not in a derogatory way, but as a term rooted in a time when we claimed our space and asserted our rights, like during the "Indian uprising." To them it's a proud declaration of "this is Indian land."

Growing up I learned that it doesn't matter what other people call me if I know who I am. After all, English words can't fully capture our identity or the depth of our teachings. I was taught that those labels don't define us, that they're just placeholders in a language that wasn't made for us. What truly matters is the connection to our teachings, our land, and each other—beyond any words the outside world might use.

Most of my intensive learning happened when I went to visit my relatives at the En'owkin Centre on our reserve, a cultural, educational, ecological and creative arts post-secondary institution that practices Indigenous knowledge and implements traditional systems. The word *en'owkin* is a conceptual metaphor in syilx that describes a process of clarification, conflict resolution, and group commitment to coming to the best solutions possible through respectful dialogue and the inclusion of all voices.

For folks looking to support the important work being done on language revitalization, climate, and ecological knowledge, I encourage you to look into their work and support it with monetary donations.[3] The work they do contributes to the well-being of all living beings and the regeneration and revitalization of lands and ecosystems based on Indigenous knowledge and language.

I was lucky to live in the same community as the En'owkin Centre because so many of our teachers and elders would spend time there, visiting, teaching, and hosting storytellers, dinners, celebrations, and honouring ceremonies. They also house Theytus Books Ltd., an Indigenous publishing company. In Salish, *theytus* means "preserving for the sake of handing down." For founder Randy Fred, it symbolizes the goal of documenting Indigenous cultures and worldviews through books.

Randy was friends with my mom and dad and was married to a woman named Edith. They were an important part of my childhood during a time when my sister and I needed a safe place to be, and I continue to stay in touch with them. Edith is a nurse and Randy continues to be involved in the writing community, and is a nuu-chah-nulth elder at Vancouver Island University.

The vice-president of the En'owkin Centre is Dr. Jeannette Armstrong, a woman I grew up around in our community and nation gatherings. My mom told me to pay attention to her. Even as a young woman she was recognized for her gifts and was often brought into spaces to speak on behalf of our elders, trusted to carry their words and teachings with care. She has spent her life listening, deeply absorbing the knowledge and wisdom of those who came before and bringing that forward in a way that honours our stories and traditions.

---

[3] https://enowkincentre.ca

There is a wisdom in her that many of our people today take for granted. Dr. Armstrong is years ahead of her time, understanding the path we need to take as a people, yet her guidance often goes unrecognized because it requires a kind of trust we've been conditioned to doubt. We live in a time where we are driven to control, to prepare, and to demand answers, traits that keep us from embracing the deep, layered guidance she offers. Her teachings require us to let go of that need for control and to have faith in each other and the journey itself, even when we don't fully understand.

It would be beautiful to see our communities come together and value each other again, even when the path isn't clear. In a perfect world we would listen and learn from each other without the constant need for clarity, trusting in the wisdom of our ancestors and the voices of those who hold our teachings. Dr. Armstrong shows us this vision: a world where our communities are grounded in genuine connection and mutual respect, where we come together in our shared strengths, and where each person's value is seen, honoured, and trusted.

Our elders from the eighties and nineties saw her value and trusted her to represent our nation's voice, knowing she held our teachings with a respect and understanding that few could comprehend. Her dedication has woven our language, medicine, and stories into the spaces that need them most—not just to preserve them, but to help them thrive in the modern world. Dr. Armstrong's work is a testament to a lifetime spent in service to our people, bridging our wisdom with the broader world while staying rooted in the land and community that shaped her. Her contributions are threaded into every part of the En'owkin Centre, alongside her brother Richard's, who is also a respected elder and teacher there.

It's a place where countless influential Indigenous leaders, artists, and creators have gathered in spaces alive with the knowledge, strength, and resilience of our people. I was fortunate to grow up learning from and witnessing in person some of the most respected and impactful voices of our time—figures like Dr. Jeannette Armstrong; Dr. Lee Maracle; Dr. Grand Chief Stewart Phillip and his wife, MLA Joan Phillip; and Gwen Phillips. These weren't just community leaders, they were internationally recognized trailblazers who influenced not only our communities but movements worldwide. Well known spiritual leaders also entered our home, bringing prophecies, teachings, and perspectives that deepened my understanding of who we are and what we carry.

A few years ago my little sister Emma-Lena lent me *Outliers* by Malcolm Gladwell. In it he talks about how success is often built on layers of opportunity, community, and timing, factors that aren't always in our control. Reading that, I thought about the people I've been able to learn from and the chances I've had as an Indigenous woman. My life has been shaped not only by my own efforts but by the presence of these remarkable people and the spaces they created. It's a reminder that we don't move forward alone; we're lifted by those who came before us and by the strength of community that surrounds us.

I was born in 1977 to a mother whose mother was a direct descendant of our hereditary chiefs. My grandmother Ellen spoke our language fluently. Born in 1904, she remembered life before settlers had a strong presence, though she likely saw them from a distance with little direct contact. I spent my first six years with her, absorbing her teachings and stories. She passed down our ways so naturally that it felt just the way life was meant to be: simple, grounded, and connected to the land.

My mom would often take my tema out for "cruises," driving her around so she could share her memories with us. My tema would point out places where she had lived as a young girl, at summer camps stretching from Spokane, Washington, all the way up to Vernon, BC, which was approximately a 415-kilometre distance. She would talk about her winter camp, an underground house in Okanagan Falls, BC. I think of the distances she covered, all without a car, travelling across a landscape that was part of who she was.

My tema even had land in Washington State. I remember finding the paperwork in my mom's files when I was in my twenties, a quiet reminder of the deep, lasting connections my tema had to the land across borders. Those drives became a journey through her memories, a way for her to pass down our family's history, the land, and the stories that have shaped us.

When I became older I would drop into the En'owkin Centre to ask about the classes and programs, and one day I signed up for Dr. Armstrong's class. She talked about spirit helpers and coming-of-age and our names. But one thing she said during that class really struck me, and it hit my body like a ton of bricks. At that moment I knew that I had been raised in a way that most people only read about.

She explained how our elders would begin guiding our children from the age of four, preparing them with teachings and experiences to deepen their connection to the land and to themselves. Sometimes children were encouraged to take on journeys alone, like following a creek to its headwaters or spending quiet time in the mountains. Sometimes our elders would gift us their spirit helpers by giving us something of theirs, like a handkerchief, before sending us out in the dark. These moments were meant to help us connect with our inner selves, to trust our instincts, and to begin finding our spirit helpers. Spirit helpers are like guardians who would support us throughout our lives. These spirit helpers, like guardian angels, offer comfort, inspiration, and reminders that we are never alone. They help build our faith in something greater than ourselves, a force that connects and guides us all.

I was thirty-one years old, just over a year sober, when I first heard Dr. Armstrong share this teaching. In that moment memories of my tema sending me on seemingly small tasks—like retrieving her handkerchief from a woodpile in the dark or going up the creek alone—rushed back to me. A wave of emotion hit me and something clicked inside. I realized that these moments, which once seemed ordinary, held something incredibly special.

Reflecting on our teachings and my mom's insistence on keeping faith in the Creator, I understand now how deeply we were raised to trust. My mom made us practice faith daily. We trusted in the Creator, in the land, in our ways, learning without needing immediate answers. Dr. Armstrong's words connected with those teachings in a way that made me feel I was hearing it at exactly the right moment, as though all my experiences had led me to this understanding right when I needed it most.

Before I finally got sober I didn't even realize that what I'd gone through as a child was trauma. At the time I blamed everything on alcohol. I started drinking when I was twelve, and from that very first drink it felt like something clicked—a quick, easy escape from feelings I didn't know how to handle. Alcohol became my way of silencing the pain and burying memories that hurt too much to face. But the thing about alcohol is that it doesn't just block out the bad memories. It numbs everything, even the good things. For years I struggled to remember the teachings my tema had shared with me, the moments of guidance and connection, because I was drowning them out with booze.

My teachers explained that alcohol has a spirit of its own, and when you drink it that spirit takes over and drives yours out. They told me that's why you feel hollow and disconnected afterward, like you've lost a piece of yourself. Drinking leaves you feeling numb, sick, and useless, a shell of who you are. Looking back I can see that every time I drank I was pushing away my spirit, disconnecting myself from the strength and wisdom my ancestors had placed in me.

I tried many times to quit because, deep down, I knew alcohol was destroying me. But I could never seem to make it past that one-year mark of sobriety. After a while without drinking, emotions I'd long buried would start to surface—anger, sadness, grief—and my body didn't know how to process them. I'd get overwhelmed by waves of anxiety because I couldn't cry. Growing up we were taught that crying was a sign of weakness, a message drilled into us from the church and residential schools. So I learned to shut down my tears, even though I could feel the pressure building up inside me. I'd sit there feeling like I was going to explode, unable to let those emotions out in the way my body needed.

When I wasn't drinking, painful memories would begin to creep back in and I didn't have the tools to handle them. Those memories were like ghosts rising from the past, things I had tried so hard to forget. And because I had never been taught how to process or heal from them, the only way I knew to escape was to reach for the bottle again. Drinking would push the memories back down where I didn't have to see them, didn't have to feel them. But each time I chose that escape I was delaying the healing that my spirit needed.

The last time I drank hard I ended up in bed for a day, still feeling drunk from the night before. I knew it was the last time I would drink. On October 10, 2007, I decided I was done. I was thirty years old. I also knew I would have to deal with the things that made me drink. I would have to work through the pain and anger and learn to forgive myself, and others, so that I could reclaim myself.

The longer I stayed sober, the more I remembered the bad things. But I also started to remember the good things, like stories my tema shared, the feeling of her warmth and safety. Random nsyilxcen would pop into my head—when I saw something I would remember the nsyilxcen word for it.

I am what is known among our people as a "silent speaker," meaning I can understand what people are saying when they speak nsyilxcen but I do not speak it myself. One time, Richard Armstrong asked me a question in the language and I responded in English. In English, he said, "You know what I'm saying when I speak nsyilxcen but you don't speak it back. How come?" I said, "I don't know. Maybe I get nervous I will say it wrong, or I get stuck in my head." He said, "I would be interested to know why that is."

The First Peoples' Cultural Council is a provincial Crown Corporation formed by the government of British Columbia in 1990. It developed the Reclaiming My Language program to help silent speakers like me.[4] Many silent speakers carry a deep, often intergenerational connection to our languages, but due to complex trauma or years of discouragement find it hard to speak aloud. This program provides a supportive space to address those mental and emotional blocks. Each participant is paired with a language-speaker mentor to guide and encourage them in speaking practice, as well as a trauma therapist to help process the underlying issues that may be preventing them from finding their voice.

This blend of language mentorship and therapeutic support acknowledges that reconnecting with language is more than just learning words, it's a journey of healing and rediscovering identity. Language carries our stories and values, and the wisdom of our ancestors. For many silent speakers, overcoming these barriers to speaking their language represents a return to self, a reclaiming of something that was never truly lost but lying dormant, waiting for the right time to be revived.

I'm interested in exploring this program more deeply one day. The idea resonates with me as I think about how much I carry within me, even if it's not always spoken aloud. For now I know that the language and teachings live in me, and even if I share them in English I'm keeping our wisdom alive and continuing that connection in a way that honours our people and our stories.

When people ask me a question, I can rarely give a quick answer. My response usually turns into a story, and I've come to realize that it's my way of sharing our language, our way of seeing the world. In our language, even one word holds so much. It's not just descriptive, it's a protocol, a law, a teaching wrapped

---

[4] fpcc.ca/program/reclaiming-my-language/

up in layers. One word can tell you not only what to do but how to carry it out, and what intentions you should hold as you do so. I'm limited in English because it doesn't do justice to our teachings. So often people try to reduce our experiences into single English words, but that language can't capture the full meaning. Our language is meant to be clear but layered, shaped by who's speaking and who they're speaking to.

In English words often mean exactly what they say, or at least that's the assumption. But in our teachings, language is layered, filled with spirit and purpose. Take "respect." In English it can simply mean politeness, but the nsyilxcen, word for respect carries responsibilities that go beyond anything English can express. In our language, respect includes a commitment to reciprocity, to our connections with everything around us. It's not just about manners, it's about recognizing that we're in a relationship with people, animals, plants, and the land itself.

If I said "respect the land" in English, it wouldn't capture the weight of our teaching. It's not about simply being kind to the land, it's about seeing the land as a living relative, honouring that relationship, understanding that our health and the land's are intertwined. It's not a concept that can be reduced to a sentence, it's something you have to feel, to see lived out, to truly understand it.

That's why our stories are long. They're layered and full of examples guiding you to the heart of what our words mean, taking you through the landscapes of our minds and hearts so you don't just *know* the teaching, you *feel* it. Every detail matters, every part of the story builds a fuller picture. When we try to make our stories short or skip over parts to make them more palatable for English speakers, something essential gets lost.

Our elders understood this. They taught us through stories that took their time because they knew that the depth and meaning couldn't be rushed. They didn't speak just to be heard, they spoke so that the words would live in us so the teachings would be carried forward whole, not in bits and pieces. If we start trimming down these teachings to fit into simpler terms we lose the heart of them, the parts that stay with you and keep you grounded. Our stories aren't just information, they're medicine, and you don't rush medicine if you want it to heal.

Our stories are long because they work to convey what our language and laws mean in a way that others can understand without misinterpretation. We can't be lazy when bringing these teachings forward. Each detail carries meaning, and the connections are essential. As I write I find myself explaining things in layers, circling back to details as they become relevant, because in our teachings everything connects. For some my writing might feel disjointed because it doesn't follow a strict, linear path; instead, it moves with the rhythm these stories were given to me. This way of sharing doesn't lack "proper" English, it's rooted in the cadence and wisdom of our ancestors. My wisdom doesn't come from following formal rules but from the ancestral knowledge and stories I carry forward.

I often share openly about my inability to succeed in school. I was lucky to get a C+ on most tests. I had a hard time focusing. From the moment I stepped foot in school I experienced discrimination and racism. I was bullied for my clothes, my skin, and the way I talked. I didn't like sitting in a classroom so I ended up skipping school and getting into fights.

I really wanted to fit in and be smart in school. I loved to read, and I wanted to be special and successful. Growing up I heard that I could only be successful if I went to school, graduated, and went to university. But every time I struggled and failed I felt like that was it, I was never going to be successful. What I knew was as good as it was going to get.

School became a place where I constantly questioned my worth. I was always looking for ways to fit in and belong, and if I couldn't I became quiet. I questioned everything I knew about who I was because I was scared to be shamed, told I was wrong or different. When I first started school I knew who I was and where I belonged. I had a strong understanding of my teachings. But by the time I turned six I didn't want to be Indigenous, and by seven I was spending hours in the bathtub trying to use soap to wash the brown off my skin because I was taught my skin made me dirty and ugly.

Coming-of-age beautifully teaches us how loved and valued we are. It tells us that because we were born we are valued. Coming-of-age rooted a deep knowing inside of us, an inner guide that helps us navigate the world. Many of our teachings were passed on in our families without us even knowing it, in the way we were parented, the way we were scolded, and the questions we were asked. This is how we learned what was important.

Coming-of-age mentoring and protocols can begin as young as four years old. It was the role of our old people to watch the babies and the children, to see the way they acted and how they were in the world. They would look for the light in our children and find ways to nurture it, to bring it forward.

My tema always sat at the kitchen table playing solitaire early in the mornings before the sun came up, and later in the evenings after dinner. When I was around four or five she would sometimes tell me to go outside and get her handkerchief from the woodpile by the old shed. I never thought to ask why she wanted it at night, I just knew she wanted it.

The shed was old, built by my grandpa in the early 1900s with my uncles' carving tools. There was a big woodpile stacked next to it about thirty-five feet from the back steps. I would push open the squeaky screen door, turn on the back-porch light, and step down to the bottom of the stairs, gripping the railing, trying to peer into the darkness around the woodpile. I'd take a step or two away from the porch but then get spooked and hurry back. I never wondered if my tema was watching from the window, but she probably was.

I'd go out there in tiny steps, listening to every sound in the night. I'd hear rustling in the field, the hoot of an owl, the creek gurgling nearby. Sometimes I'd run back inside and grab my tema's big green flashlight, rushing back out to shine it towards the woodpile, squinting to see her handkerchief. I'd stand there, feeling the cool night air, but then a shiver would run down my spine and I'd turn and sprint back into the house, heart racing, all the little hairs on my arms standing up. My tema would laugh when I came back empty-handed, and I'd go back to sitting with her as she played her game of cards. Or sometimes I'd run to the living room and jump on my Uncle Louie's back while he watched sports or *Cheers*, feeling safe with him until I eventually fell asleep, and he'd wait for someone to carry me to bed.

Years later I understood that these little tasks were about more than fetching a handkerchief: my tema was teaching me courage. This was her way of helping me connect with my spirit helper, preparing me to stand in the dark and face the fear, to know that I could hold steady even when everything in me wanted to turn and run.

When I got older my mom explained that when you feel that shiver run up your spine, it's a sign of your spirit helper drawing near. We're taught to stand still and welcome it, not to run. Our elders were training us to face fear, to know that we could withstand it. In the same way they had us endure the heat of sweat lodges to prepare for summer and jump into ice-cold water to strengthen us for winter. They knew that if we could meet fear and discomfort head-on we would be resilient.

Science now backs up what our people have always known. Studies show that exposure to cold, like jumping into icy water, triggers a survival response that strengthens the nervous system, increases circulation, and releases endorphins, natural chemicals that boost our mood and resilience. Cold-water immersion, now recognized for its mental health benefits, has long been a practice in our culture, not for physical conditioning alone but to build our spirits and our minds. Scientists are now learning that cold exposure can increase our ability to handle stress and even enhance our immune systems.

Similarly, enduring the heat of a sweat lodge or extreme warmth conditions the body and mind in powerful ways. Heat therapy, now studied for its benefits, has been shown to improve cardiovascular health, reduce inflammation, and promote the release of proteins that repair cells. But for our people it wasn't just about physical endurance, it was a spiritual preparation, teaching us to sit with discomfort, to trust in our strength, and to connect to something greater.

Our teachings taught us to respect these elements as sacred, not just physical challenges but as a way to build resilience, to learn how to stay calm in the face of fear. This understanding was built into our language and stories, the teachings we passed down to make each generation stronger. What colonial Western science now validates about stress tolerance, mental resilience, and physical benefits was already woven into our culture as essential knowledge.

Now when people tell me I'm courageous, I think back to those nights outside my tema's house. I realize that courage isn't the absence of fear, it's about learning to stand in it, to let it wash over you and know you're not alone. My tema's quiet teachings prepared me to face the unknown, to trust that even in the darkness I carry the strength of those who came before me. They understood that resilience comes from pushing through fear, not avoiding it, and that every lesson from the land, the cold and the heat, was there to remind us of the strength we already hold.

Reflecting on these teachings I feel a deep sense of loss for the practices that once held our people strong and steady. Our ancestors knew how to build resilience by guiding us through discomfort rather than protecting us from it. They taught us to work with fear, heat, and cold to see them not as threats but as teachers, each one shaping our capacity to endure. But when these practices were taken away, so too was the strength they gave us, the foundation that allowed us to weather hardship with grace and self-regulation.

Without these practices we've become vulnerable to being easily overwhelmed, quick to anger, quick to retreat. Many of us now find it hard to sit with discomfort or handle stress. We look for ways to avoid pressure rather than move through it. I see how this impacts our communities, how the lack of these teachings has made us more sensitive, more easily triggered. Our systems—physical, mental, spiritual—aren't as equipped to withstand life's challenges, and we often find ourselves reactive rather than resilient.

I think about the times we're living in, how modern society encourages us to escape or numb our pain, to seek quick fixes rather than face what's uncomfortable. But our elders knew there is strength to be found in discomfort. They taught us that resilience is cultivated, not given, and that facing our fears was essential to understanding our own power. When we don't have that foundation we feel adrift in times of struggle, reaching for anything that might make the pain easier to bear.

It's easy to forget that ancient practices of resilience and connection to the land aren't limited to the Indigenous cultures we recognize today. They're rooted in so many of our human histories across lands and generations. These aren't just our teachings, they're universal.

In Nordic countries, for example, cold plunges and sauna rituals have been around for centuries, guiding people to respect the power of the elements. Nordic and Russian cultures have long embraced this balance between ice and fire, with people moving from icy waters to the intense heat of saunas. It's not just a physical ritual, it's spiritual too. It's a practice to cleanse, to renew, and to build strength, a knowledge passed down about how to be resilient in the face of nature's extremes.

The British Isles also have these deep-rooted practices. The Scots have the Highland games, but they're not just about competition, they're about pushing yourself, building endurance, and sharing that strength with the community. The games became a space to gather, to celebrate resilience, to strengthen bonds through shared challenges. The Welsh have *gwyllt*, an awe and reverence for the wild, untamed places. The wilderness isn't just a landscape to them, it is a teacher, a source of inner strength. When people gather around the fires of Beltane (the Gaelic May Day festival) in Scotland and Wales, they aren't just marking a change of seasons, they are engaging in a ritual that transforms them, preparing them to face whatever comes next with courage. Fire is their strength, just as water and cold are for Scandinavians.

It's a powerful reminder that these values of courage, resilience, and respect for nature live in all of us. The countries we now think of as colonizers also have their own Indigenous ways of being, their own deep-rooted wisdom that values harmony with the land. Colonial history has buried some of these traditions but they're still there, a thread of memory in our stories, waiting for us to remember them. We all come from people who honoured these things, who knew how to gather strength from the land and each other. These teachings are gifts that each culture holds, and they are not there to be validated by science, but to be remembered and honoured in our own ways.

Imagine if we could return to those teachings, if we could reclaim our relationship with discomfort as a way to strengthen ourselves. How differently might we approach stress or loss? Instead of crumbling under pressure we might stand firm, knowing we carry the strength of our ancestors within us. This loss of our practices isn't just about missing traditions, it's about losing a vital part of what kept us whole.

For me, reconnecting with these teachings is a reminder of our true resilience and a call to reawaken it. It's about remembering that our capacity to endure has always been there, waiting to be tapped into. And it's a challenge to all of us to push through the discomfort, to face our fears, and to trust that, in doing so, we are reclaiming the strength that was always ours.

The things I've come to learn about science and the brain don't *validate* me or my people's knowledge. Our teachings, our ways, have always held their own truth. This science merely confirms what we've known all along. For generations our people understood resilience, healing, and the power of connecting to the land and spirit in ways that modern science is only now beginning to recognize. It's as if the world is just catching up to the wisdom that was always there, rooted deeply in our ways of being.

As I've come to trust myself and my stories, I've also learned to uphold my teachings in everything I do, including this journey of writing. I'm often asked to validate what I share, to reference where I learned something, to back up my thinking with data. But my teachings don't come from books or studies, they come from the lived experience of being in community, from the stories and knowledge passed down through countless interactions with elders, family, and mentors. At times I reference something I've read or someone who has influenced me because acknowledging our teachers is essential. But so many people have shaped me, and these teachings flow through me as naturally as my breath.

Our elders gifted us this practice of building strength and resilience from a young age. Little by little, from as early as four years old, we were taught to face fear, to grow confident in ourselves. When we learn to stand in our fear we build a trust in ourselves that allows us to move through life with courage. This is a powerful teaching that allows us to do things others may hold back from because they don't have that foundation of trust.

Consider your own journey. Were you encouraged to confront fear or to sidestep it? Are you able to show up fully in challenging spaces without seeking to soften the discomfort? And how do you begin to rebuild or deepen your trust in yourself, allowing space for fear yet moving forward with resilience?

I remember asking one of my teachers, "What does it mean when I see my spirit helper all the time?" He answered, "It means the Creator loves you so much that they sent them to watch over you, to remind you that you are loved." That fills my heart, knowing that we are supported in ways we can't always see. Our children used to be born into a world where they would hear our language from birth, surrounded by messages that they belonged, that they were loved. What a gift that was.

Chapter 10

LITTLE SIBLING AND PATIENCE

In one of our syilx stories, the Creator gives the first two Animal People, Coyote and his twin brother Fox, laws to live by:

> As the Creator was preparing the world, he told the siblings that they were going to receive a gift. The Creator then told the twins that one of them would receive a book. The Creator placed it on a rock and told them that, when they came back together, it would be decided who would receive the book.
>
> The older twin, Coyote, began hunting and keeping busy, but the younger one, Fox, stuck around and decided that he was going to take the book because he knew Coyote would earn it. So Fox stole the book, and when the Creator came back he denied the theft. The Creator told Fox to take the book to a small puddle and jump to the other side without touching the water. Fox did what he was told. When he landed, he turned around and all he could see was a large body of water, which is now the Atlantic Ocean.
>
> The Creator told Fox to use the knowledge in the book to find his way back across the large

body of water to be reunited with Coyote. Coyote was instructed to walk the land to prepare for a time when Fox would return.

Fox was so burdened by the weight of the knowledge he had to learn to cross the water that he forgot about the land teachings altogether.

When Fox returned, he brought a series of laws that disregarded the natural laws of the world, and it has become the responsibility of Coyote and his people to re-teach the laws of the land.

The first time I heard this story I was a little girl sitting among syilx elders as they talked about governments and agreements. They spoke of how the government was always trying to find ways to break the agreements that recognized our right to access our lands, practice our customs, and uphold our sovereignty. In these discussions our people would talk about how to respond when those in government didn't seem to understand our ways.

The elders would often say, "You know how younger siblings are. Sometimes you need to be patient with them and teach them things they don't understand yet." They weren't saying this to dismiss or look down on the government representatives, but to remind us that we are on different paths. As older siblings, our role is not to judge or resent but to hold our ground with patience and offer guidance. The little sibling isn't lesser, they just carry a different understanding, one that might need time and gentleness to find alignment with our teachings.

Growing up I often heard different ideas about people who worked in government. On one hand I was taught to be patient, to view them as "little siblings" who had wandered far from natural teachings and might need reminders of a different way. On the other hand I was warned that government workers were often hardened by the system, caught up in rules that pulled them away from their own humanity. I was told that in their roles, many people forget how to listen to the land, instead serving laws in books while the laws of the land sit forgotten.

Over the years I have witnessed Grand Chief Stewart Phillip's approach to working with our communities, our nation, and our leadership across the country, as well as government representatives. His messaging is always strong and firm in asserting our title and rights, delivered from an understanding that love is the only answer. At a past meeting, provincial government representatives were delivering their well-planned-out messaging, and our First Nations leadership began attacking them. You could feel fear and discomfort creeping into the room.

When it was Grand Chief Stewart Phillip's turn to address the assembly, he spoke eloquently and from the heart, as he always does, ending with, "We have to remember to be hard on systems and soft on people." His comment stayed with me as I learned to navigate my own anger and pain when it came to dealing with government representatives.

Government systems to promote fear and control have been in place for over 150 years in Canada. These systems are not "broken," they are doing what they were always meant to do: keep us in a place of fear. When we are scared we can lose hope, and hopeless people are easy to control.

I started working with provincial and federal governments at the age of twenty-three as a subcontractor for the Ministry of Health. When I was twenty-nine I was chosen as an intern for the pilot year of the Indigenous Youth Internship Program (formerly the Aboriginal Youth Internship Program), and I was placed with the Ministry of Children and Family Development. In 2008 I worked as an employee for the federal government in Indigenous Services Canada, in the Community Initiatives Unit.

Over those first two decades of my experience I began to have a clear understanding of how things worked internally and externally. I started to understand their processes and policies, and to see the places where fear lives within them. When you work within a system or a group of people for long enough it's easy to get pulled into the culture, to start moving with the current instead of questioning it. I knew I had to go back home and visit with my elders and teachers every two weeks to keep me grounded and focused, to remind myself why I was there and who I was accountable to.

Our governments and corporations thrive on colonial systems of fear, and they are designed to keep people locked in what I call "fear brain." Neuroscience shows us that when our brains perceive a threat—whether it's a real, physical danger or a subtle fear of stepping outside the norms—the amygdala, the brain's fear centre, takes over. In this survival state our brains can't access the prefrontal cortex, the executive brain, the part that governs creativity, complex thinking, and long-term planning. We fall into survival mode and become focused on following routines and avoiding risk. Colonial systems capitalize on this by creating rigid processes that allow people to operate automatically, relying on pre-set responses and procedures rather than critical thinking.

When people are in this fear-driven mode they lose the capacity to challenge the status quo. They can't ask bigger questions or step outside their comfort zones because the brain simply doesn't function that way under stress. Instead they stick to the script, reciting protocols and recycling the same ideas and solutions in every new situation. It's a system designed to keep people feeling safe, but that safety is just an illusion that prevents real growth, creativity, and meaningful change. When we operate out of fear we're using only a fraction of our potential, just enough to keep the system running without upsetting its balance.

This fear-brain approach is why executive leaders and mid-management often cause the biggest bottlenecks to change. Although they're positioned to lead and make decisions, they end up becoming some of the most risk-averse people in the organization. They are constantly answering to people above them who expect them to uphold the system and deliver results, while also managing people below them who are relying on them to provide direction. This pressure from both directions pushes them further into a fear-based mindset, where maintaining control and avoiding risk becomes more important than fostering innovation or progress.

To feel in control these leaders often cling to policies, rules, and protocols, not just to guide others but as a form of self-protection. By reinforcing these systems they create the sense that everything is under control, even if it's stifling creativity and making real solutions impossible. They may not realize it but this fear of challenging the system ultimately holds them back from leading in a meaningful way. Their fear becomes contagious, setting a tone of rigidity and inaction that trickles down through the whole organization, reinforcing the cycle of compliance and inaction.

When I think about the story of the younger and older siblings, I see the parallels clearly. The younger sibling took the book, separating themselves from the land and the teachings of our people. They returned with a knowledge that created division instead of connection, building laws and systems that ignored the natural ways.

The same dynamic plays out in colonial systems. Rules and protocols take the place of real understanding, and fear keeps people from connecting with each other and the larger purpose of their work. But just like in our teachings, it's our role to practice patience with the "little sibling" who has wandered off track. We have a responsibility to re-teach the natural laws, to bring back that balance by helping people see beyond the fear and rigid systems. Imagine what could change if we could help each other out of this fear brain, if we could bring people back into a state of creativity, connection, and trust in themselves and each other.

This fear-driven structure doesn't just impact government officials and corporate leaders, it filters down to our elected

Indigenous leadership, our chiefs and councils. They sit in a complicated position, expected by our people to bring change, to fight for resources, and to protect our rights. Our communities look to them with hope, expecting them to be able to fix everything. But the reality is, within the colonial system much of their power is just that: perceived.

Our chiefs and councils are bound by federal government rules that dictate how funding is allocated for essential areas like social development, education, and housing. To keep these programs running they are required to operate within strict guidelines that the federal government sets, which are often out of touch with the real needs of our communities. So while our people are asking them to create real change, to address the deep-rooted issues in our communities, they're often left with limited options, navigating a system that was never designed for us to thrive.

Our people don't always see these limitations. They see our leaders advocating and attending meetings, and they assume those conversations will bring immediate results. When nothing changes the frustration often lands on the shoulders of our chiefs and councils, who are seen as the ones in power. But it's a constrained power, constantly checked by rules, reporting structures, and funding requirements that ultimately serve to keep them and, by extension, all of us dependent on the federal system. We've been given a seat at the table without a real voice in the decisions being made.

When our leaders approach the government to demand better conditions for our people, they are met with officials who are themselves bound by a fear-based culture. Government representatives, from middle management to the top, feel pressure from every side: the public, their own supervisors, and Indigenous leaders who demand action.

Often they don't know how to respond to our leaders because they are so deeply entrenched in the system's protocols, unable to step outside their own fear of making mistakes, losing control, or offending someone above them. They operate in this guarded, defensive space, reinforcing the policies they've been taught to uphold rather than seeking real solutions.

In the end what we get is two groups: the government officials and our elected leaders, each under immense pressure but unable to move beyond the confines of a system built on fear and control. Our chiefs and councils come into these negotiations wanting to do right by our people only to be met with a colonial system so tangled in its own fear-based practices that it can't truly engage with us. When our people see this stagnation the frustration continues to build, reinforcing the perception that our leaders are failing or not fighting hard enough.

This cycle of perceived power and constrained authority creates division within our communities. We end up turning our frustrations inward, often directing them at the very people who are trying to help us navigate this broken system. Our leaders carry the weight of our expectations, but they're walking through a landscape full of barriers and boundaries that were set long before any of us arrived at the table.

Reflecting on the story of Coyote and Fox, I see the parallels in this struggle. The younger sibling, Fox, burdened by the book of knowledge and disconnected from the teachings of the land, brought a structure of control and disconnection that now governs everything. Some of our elected leaders are like Coyote, trying to bring our teachings and values into this colonial space to honour our connection to the land and our people, while navigating a system that isn't designed to understand or respect those values. Like the story reminds us, our work is to practice patience. Not only with the system, but with ourselves and each other, remembering that this isn't a simple path but one that requires us to keep walking, even when it feels impossible.

Coming-of-age is a process that doesn't just shape individuals, it reconnects us to our roots, to who we are and where we come from, grounding us in purpose. It strengthens the confidence we need to contribute meaningfully, to show up as our best selves. As my friend David Dennis, whom I mentioned earlier in this book, wisely said, "It's not just our babies that need coming-of-age. It's all of us. We all have to remember who we are."

Coming-of-age as a leader means developing the resilience to do what's right even when people are pressuring, questioning, or attacking them to do better. It requires a grounded sense of self and purpose so they can hold steady in the face of criticism and high expectations. True leadership isn't just about delivering answers on demand, it's about being able to hold space for complexity, to move forward with integrity, and to act from a place of vision rather than reaction.

For government leaders, executives, and others working within high-pressure systems, this means knowing that sometimes doing better involves moving through the discomfort of not having immediate solutions, of choosing a path that isn't guaranteed.

Leaders who have come of age understand that the real strength lies in navigating this discomfort with patience and empathy without letting fear or outside pressure drive their decisions. They stay true to the purpose of self-determination, for themselves and those they serve, by leading in a way that empowers others to trust their own journeys, even when the path is uncertain.

In the end this grounded approach allows leaders to stay focused on what truly matters: creating space for growth, fostering resilience, and cultivating a sense of belonging that transcends fear and control.

So how do we help our little siblings remember their humanness, especially when they're part of a system that has colonized, controlled, and oppressed us all? It's a delicate task. They need to learn to be hard on the system, questioning it, challenging it, but soft on people. Each of us has a role to play in this.

If you've ever had a younger sibling, you know how much work and patience it takes to teach them something important.

It takes repetition and storytelling to help them absorb and carry the teachings forward. Our natural laws can't be taught in a single lesson. They're learned through the stories, experiences, and values that shape who we are over time.

It can be frustrating when a younger sibling isn't listening. Sometimes we lose our patience, and we might even yell at or scold them, thinking that will make them understand. But we know where that leads. When people are met with anger and punishment they shut down, rebel, or act out. They stop feeling safe, loved, and connected, and retreat into the emotional parts of their brain where information doesn't stick.

They might move into a place of cynicism and hopelessness or act from the survival brain stem, the part that just wants to escape and survive. In this state they're more likely to make mistakes and become stuck in cycles that don't serve anyone.

Being patient with people, especially those who have contributed to harmful systems that impact our families, can be one of the hardest things we do. But when I think of our ancestors, our elders, and teachers, I am reminded of the depth of patience they extended to us. They would say, "They just don't know any better," as a reminder to lead with empathy. I try to remember that as I teach and advocate, and it gives me the strength to approach others with patience.

When we teach and lead with patience and love, sharing stories that resonate with people's hearts and emotions, we help them reconnect with their own humanness. In times of anger, remembering our teachings, drawing on that well of patience, can completely shift the direction of a meeting or gathering. It allows each voice to be heard and gives everyone the opportunity to contribute to changing the harmful systems that make us forget our humanness in the first place.

Our traditional syilx stories guide us in the importance of all voices. Every circle must include diverse perspectives, experiences, and concerns, bringing balance through the wisdom of many ways of seeing. Practicing the discipline to listen deeply to one another brings about an awakening, a reminder that we are all connected. In that connection we find a sense of safety and belonging that allows us to work from a place of creativity, resilience, and collective strength.

I know that for many of us the patience called for by these teachings can feel challenging, especially in the face of relentless injustices. It's frustrating for those within these systems, and even more so for those looking in from the outside, seeing the harm they cause and the slow pace of change. That anger, that sense of being fed up, is valid and rooted in real harm. But our teachings remind us that this patience isn't about passivity, it's about staying grounded and moving forward with strength so we don't let our own spirits be consumed by these systems.

As Dr. Jeannette Armstrong writes in her essay "En'owkin: What It Means to Be a Sustainable Community," published in 2005 by the Centre for Ecoliteracy, "When we include the perspective of the land and of human relationships in our decisions, people in the community change. Material things and all the worrying about matters such as money start to lose their power. When people realize the community is there to sustain them, they have the most secure feeling in the world. The fear starts to leave, and they are imbued with hope" (Armstrong, 2005, p. 17).

In times of frustration and fatigue we can lean into this truth: our community, our land, and our teachings are here to sustain us, to keep us moving forward, even when the way forward isn't clear.

In these challenging times, when frustration and anger feel overwhelming, what small ways can you reconnect to your community, your values, or the land to remind yourself of the strength that sustains you? How can you use that connection to find hope and continue moving forward, even when the path seems difficult?

Chapter 11

PEOPLE-EATERS

Before humans were here there were People-Eaters. People-Eaters were beings that were not able to live in harmony with all other living beings. The Animal People knew that the People-to-Be would be coming and that they had to start preparing the land for them. The land was changed to leave laws and stories for the People-to-Be so that they would know how to govern themselves and take care of the land so that it would always regenerate.

Coyote was sn'klip, the trickster, and the Creator gave sn'klip powers to change the land and shapeshift to get it prepared, to make sure the land was safe for the People-to-Be. People-Eaters came in the form of giants, horses, owls, mosquitos, and other creatures. Sn'klip travelled the lands to find them and would often trick them or find other ways to transform them into something that would be useful. Sometimes they were transformed into something that humans still use today, and sometimes they were transformed as a lesson to share.

When I started doing work with governments and people whose ideas and thinking were opposite to mine, my cousin Lauren told me, "Remember the teachings of sn'klip and the People-Eaters. The intention is never to destroy something, it is to transform them into something that is useful."

My mom used to take me to protest roadblocks, where we'd bring supplies to support those standing on the front lines. I'd attend occupations of government buildings and help organize rallies to raise awareness of the violence and desecration being inflicted on our sacred lands through unchecked development, happening without the consultation of our nations.

For many years I was deeply involved in direct action and frontline advocacy. I wanted to follow in the footsteps of my dad, who was always at the forefront, shutting things down. I listened to our passionate leaders from all backgrounds, many of whom would say that the only way forward was to tear down these systems, that they had to be destroyed. It made me pause and reconsider my approach, especially as I remembered the words of an elder I'd heard at an Indigenous political meeting.

He stood up and said, "Do not tear down existing systems. That thinking supports the systems that we want to change. When we do things from our ways, we think, *What do we need to do to feed the field, how do we nurture?* The system is definitely broken, and I will always work towards positive change, but you will never see me fight against something, because when we protest we are creating incohesiveness, and in order to change the system we have to work towards building cohesiveness." We cannot become like them if we want to do things different.

Our elders have said, "Our world now has a different kind of People-Eater, the things that do not live in harmony with all living things. The things that do not support regeneration of living things. The things that wipe out our relatives that do not speak for themselves, the plants, the animals, the water." How do we transform those things so they're useful? How do we go about finding ways to do work in a way that upholds the original teachings of these lands?

Colonization created a society of People-Eaters. Even my own people have become People-Eaters, because many of us have forgotten who we are. We have started to make decisions based on what we want as humans to make things easier and more comfortable for us, not based on what is best for the environment.

We believe we are the most important part of the ecosystem, which goes against natural law.

Coming-of-age helps us adapt to what the land gives us. Back when it was common practice it helped us understand we were part of a system we could not control, and we as humans had to adapt to what the land gave us. Coming-of-age training teaches us to practice patience and discipline and the ability to regulate ourselves when things around us are uncomfortable. It teaches us to adapt the way we live to suit the environment.

One of Evelyn's favourite stories is about the time sn'klip challenged the Creator. The Creator gave sn'klip all their powers to help prepare the world for the People-to-Be, and one day they get into an argument. Sn'klip believed they were older, smarter, and more powerful, and began to demonstrate this by moving the trees and lakes and even a mountain, but the Creator took sn'klip's powers away so he wasn't able to move them back to their original places. My mom used to tell this story to us when we were younger to keep us humble. You are not powerful because you are old and smart. You are powerful if you remember to give back or put back what you take. If you take and take the world cannot regenerate. Just because you can move mountains and redirect lakes and cut down trees doesn't mean you should.

My husband Ryan always tells me, "Just because you're good at something doesn't mean you should do it." In our stories of the four siblings, the white sibling was given the gift of fire. They mastered it, learned how to build things, and created the Industrial Revolution. They used their gift to get power. Just because you have ability and smarts to do something doesn't mean you should, and the land speaks. It shows us what happens when we don't put things back, and that as humans we do not have the power at all. Everything on this earth can live without us, but we cannot live without other living things. We are dependent on our parents, the Animal People, who gave up their lives for us.

Around 1990 I had a dream I was standing on top of the hill on the Penticton Indian Band reserve overlooking the city. There were hundreds of bears lying across the rolling hills and I knew the end of the world was coming. I knew that things were going to change. I dreamt that I ran down Westhills Drive to where it meets Green Mountain Road and hid in a cabin that was placed at the intersection of that road and the creek. As I sat against the wall with my knees pulled up to my chest I saw bears circling the cabin, four of them, and one was a silvertip grizzly.

Then I was back at the top of the hill and the bears were gone and there was an army of people running up the hill towards us. Someone raised a gun and shot me in the chest. I remember the feeling of the bullet entering my body and the way I felt as I fell to the ground. I knew I was dying but didn't feel pain. I felt a sense of peace wash over me and I started gliding, almost flying, from treetop to treetop, bending my knees as much as I could so I could get more air.

When I woke up I knew the dream was an important one to remember. The bears were reminding us about our agreements and teachings. In the summer and fall of 2023 I started seeing pictures of bears all over Facebook. One was a photo from northern British Columbia of five or six bears in one tree. There were photos of bears walking the streets in towns and cities all over British Columbia and reports of black bears showing up where they never had before, including a "lost" black bear photographed in Churchill, Manitoba.

In September of 2023 a friend from my home community posted a photograph of four bears forming a circle. It was taken at the bottom of Westhills Drive where it connects with Green Mountain Road along the creek, in the same place that I had dreamed thirty-three years before.

I told my kids that Chief Black Bear is telling us something, and we better start listening.

Chapter 12

NO ONE LISTENS THESE DAYS

"Things are going to get worse before they get better, because no one listens these days." These words have been repeated by elders at various gatherings I've attended over the years. Sometimes it was at powwow, a ceremony, or a gathering when elders were given the opportunity to speak.

Every time they would say hard times were coming and to prepare ourselves as much as we could. They would tell us to remember our stories and teachings, which would sustain us. Our teachings remind us to love and forgive each other, not to forget each other and carry hate in our hearts. These things help us to listen and learn from each other.

> We were given instructions on how to live and how to behave and we've strayed away from those original instructions. What we're finding in the world today, through the signs that nature is offering us, is that we need to reflect on our behaviour—on how we're treating life and how we're treating each other as human beings. It's really parallel to the Mayan calendar when they talk of the new cycle that's coming and then you hear so much talk about the end of the world. The end of the world can also be understood as

we're being given an opportunity to put an end to our negative behaviours. These changes are going to be somewhat difficult for those that have lived the materialistic life because this new life the elders are talking about is a return to laying down values and principles that whatever we create in our life must be grounded with those values. The principles of our understanding, of the survival of the people, have always been based on peace, harmony, and respect for all of life.

— Elder Dave Courchene Jr.

Storytellers, medicine people, and prophecy people have gathered from across the world over the last few decades to share their teachings with others as they were instructed. Our stories remind us that the way we treat ourselves and each other is always reflected in what is happening on the land.

Our elders talked about a time when things would get hard, and they always shared about the importance of listening to our elders and teachings. Coming-of-age taught us how to listen from a place of discipline. As children we were brought to places where adults and elders were talking and sharing stories and we were instructed to sit quietly and pay attention to what was being said.

We were taught to listen to everyone in the room, even the people we didn't like, even the ones we didn't agree with, and to listen even if what was being said didn't make sense to us. As you get older and reflect on how you listen, it becomes apparent that this is a skill we have forgotten.

Colonial systems uphold exclusion, and a good way to begin excluding is by not listening to others. We have been taught that there is a right way and wrong way, a good way and bad way, and that "my way is always the right way," so we only listen to the people who think and act like us. I only like to listen to the people I understand, because when I don't understand something

I feel like I've been left out, or I feel stupid if I don't understand something.

Colonial systems have taught us to listen, to respond with an answer. We think we must know it all. We get scared that we're going to be tested about how well we listened and learned. When someone comes to us with a problem we aren't fully listening because we are worried about what we are supposed to say to make them feel better. We believe we have the power and responsibility to fix that person instead of simply listening with discipline.

When we listen with discipline we help the distraught person feel loved and connected, allowing them to tap into their creativity and innovation. From that place they know what they need to do to take care of themselves. When people find the answer themselves they are more likely to act on it.

Disciplined listening is a sacred gift to have. People tie the act of listening to feeling loved and respected. When I feel listened to I also feel loved and respected and connected and safe. When I don't feel listened to I feel dismissed. When people know they are being listened to it lights up their mind and spirit and they become inspired to connect. They are willing to share their ideas and gifts with you.

When we listen to every voice, every perspective, every idea in the room, it adds to our collective knowledge and wisdom so we can make better decisions. You don't have to understand a story or its meaning, you don't have to decipher it in the moment, you must only listen with an open heart and mind and allow the teachings to come into your being.

Times are going to get tougher, and we must remember to listen to each other even when we don't understand what is being shared.

Chapter 13

FREEDOM

Eagle was very fast. He raced all the Animal People and beat them. Even Fox and Wolf lost. All the people who lost these races became Eagle's slaves. Eagle was chief of all the animals, except for Turtle, who lived with his partner Muskrat. They were free because they were the only ones who did not race Eagle. They knew they could not run very fast, but one night Turtle had a dream. He was told, "You must race Eagle tomorrow to free the Animal People. They must be free when the People-to-Be come."

In the morning, Turtle told Muskrat, "Get up! Go for a swim! Get ready! We must race Eagle."

"You cannot beat him, Turtle!" Muskrat said unhappily. "He flies too fast."

"I know. All of our people lost before, but my dream told me to race and win," Turtle replied.

Together the two friends went to Eagle's camp. Turtle told Eagle, "I want to race with you tomorrow."

"All right, Turtle," Eagle answered. "Tomorrow, we race when the sun comes up. If you win, the Animal People are yours."

"Yes," Turtle agreed.

"If I win, Turtle, I will keep you here. You are betting your life on this race."

As Turtle crawled away all the Animal People laughed, because they did not think they would ever be free.

Next day, Turtle met Eagle for the race. Eagle told him, "Choose your place, Turtle. I will race you any distance you decide."

"Any place?" Turtle asked.

Eagle replied, "Our people hear me. Any place, Turtle."

Quickly Turtle said, "Then carry me up in the air, Eagle. I will tell you when to drop me. From there we will race. Whoever reaches the ground first wins the race."

Eagle began to get worried. He took Turtle high up. When Turtle yelled "Let go!" Eagle dropped him. He fell like a rock.

Eagle tried to catch up to him. Turtle stuck out his head. "E-e-eee! Hurry, Eagle! I will beat you!" The Turtle pulled in his head and fell faster. The Animal People watched. They all shouted for Turtle. Muskrat jumped around and his tail whipped the air. His partner was winning. Eagle was close! He thought, *Turtle will hit the ground like a rock.*

Turtle did, but he stood up and told the Animal People, "Now I will be Chief in making this decision. You are free. Go where you like, Animal People. Anywhere!"

The Animal People scattered. They would tell the People-to-Be about the first races. Turtle said to Eagle, "You know, I cannot always beat you, but I had a dream and I learned how to beat you. I will never overtake your speed. You will always be the fastest one. You will always catch what you want to eat. When the People-to-Be come they will dream too, and they will learn from their dreams, just as I did."

Turtle and Muskrat knew they couldn't beat Eagle by racing on his terms. They weren't fast or powerful in the way Eagle was. But they also didn't let that stop them. They leaned into their own way of being, moving forward with the wisdom Turtle received in his dream. When Turtle dreamed, he knew he had to prepare himself, to jump into the water and immerse himself in a kind of quiet strength and clarity.

In our teachings that act of preparing oneself, especially for something that feels beyond our reach, is powerful. "Preparing" in our teachings is not just a matter of getting ready in a practical sense, like it often means in English. When we say "prepare," we're talking about something deeper, something layered.

It means to ready yourself in every way, to align your emotions, mind, body, and spirit with the journey ahead. Preparing is an act of respect and intention. It's about showing up fully, honouring the process by grounding yourself emotionally, by clearing your mind and strengthening your body, and by connecting with something greater than yourself.

These acts aren't just physical, they're a way of connecting to our teachings, of cleansing ourselves from doubt and distraction and aligning with the strength and clarity we need to move forward. When Turtle prepared by jumping in the water, it was a way of readying himself not only for the race but for the responsibility that came with it, a way of connecting with his inner resilience and purpose.

When we prepare, we're not just "getting ready," we're transforming ourselves into the person who can face whatever lies ahead. We're building the inner strength to stand firm, to hold our ground, and to walk our path with intention and heart.

It's how we teach our children to face what might seem impossible by reminding them of their inner gifts and the importance of the journey itself.

When the other Animal People mocked Turtle, it wasn't just a dismissal of him as slow or incapable. It was a reflection of the hopelessness that had taken hold of them over time. The Animal People had come to accept Eagle's rule, to believe that freedom wasn't even a possibility because they couldn't see beyond the limitations placed on them. They didn't understand that Turtle's power came not from speed but from his connection to his dreams and his willingness to take a different approach.

For so many of us, colonial systems have done the same thing. We've been conditioned to believe that we're not strong enough, fast enough, or capable enough to create real change. These systems have taught us to doubt our gifts, to question our dreams, and to stay within the limits set by someone else's rules. Over generations we've been made to feel that this is the only way to live, the only path available to us. But Turtle's story reminds us that there is always another way, that our dreams and inner wisdom hold the power to guide us toward freedom.

But Turtle's story reminds us that freedom and hope don't come from fighting the same way others do. Our strength comes from honouring who we are, from following the dreams and teachings that were passed down to us. Decolonizing isn't about going back to how things used to be, it's about bringing forward the best of what we know, letting those teachings guide us as we remember how to live in harmony with each other, the land, and ourselves.

We may not be able to change everything overnight, and we may not be able to change others, but we can inspire each other to dream, to hope, and to believe in our power to create a better path forward. That's what Turtle and Muskrat showed us: when we lean into our own ways and strengths, we can find freedom on our own terms.

Think about ways you have felt limited or boxed in by systems that don't reflect who you are. How can you reconnect with your inner strength, your dreams, to create your own path, even if others don't see it or understand it yet? What dreams are calling you to act from a place of true freedom?

Chapter 14

THE COURAGE TO BE OURSELVES

While I haven't included the full story here, it is an important one—deeply tied to our histories, our relationships with the land, and the laws that have guided our people for generations[5]. Part of my own coming-of-age journey has been about claiming my dad's blood, which is also mine, connecting me to the secwépemc people. These are my stories and teachings too. There's a deep sense of belonging that comes from knowing I'm not only tied to this history through my father but through countless connections, back and forth across the generations. This journey of reclaiming my secwépemc roots has been about embracing the fullness of who I am, accepting that these teachings are part of my life, my identity, and my responsibility to carry forward.

In bringing this story into my writing I'm acknowledging that I'm here because of these ties, because of the lives that have crisscrossed these lands and stitched us together. These stories flow through me, grounding me in my dad's teachings and those of our shared ancestors. Coming-of-age for me is about walking forward with all of it, honouring every part of who I am and knowing that these stories are as much mine to carry as they were for those who came before.

---

[5] The full story can be found in *Secwépemc People, Land, and Laws: Yerí7 re Stsq'ey's-kucw* by Marianne Ignace and Ronald E. Ignace.

On one side of a snowy mountain were Bird People led by Swan, who was their chief, and on the other side of the mountain were the Deer People, and their chief was Elk.

They were enemies for a long time, and they were always interfering with each other's business and had a hard time building up their food stores. They had different ways of doing things, governing, and living.

What one group did well the other did poorly, and they all suffered. One group would try to act like the other. The Winged People tried to act like the Four-Legged, and the Four-Legged tried to act like the Winged, and they were pitiful.

Swan wanted to figure out how to fix things so they could be good to each other. They believed the people were stubborn and that was why they were being troublesome and a nuisance to one another.

One winter day Swan asked one of his people to go over the mountain and invite Elk to come, and whoever did so would be paid lots of dentalium, a type of seashell used in making jewellery. Coyote said he would go, but he did not want to walk in the deep snow so he waited, saying he would go the next day. When people asked why he didn't go, he said he was practicing running and would go the next day. The next day Coyote tried to go but the snow was too deep, so he came back and fell asleep. They asked him again and he said he was practicing running.

Finally Swan asked his relatives who the fittest one was, and they said Porcupine always walks in the snowy mountains in the deep snow.

Coyote made fun of Porcupine's short legs, but Porcupine went anyway. Porcupine made it over the snowy mountain and gave Elk the message from Swan.

The next day Elk arrived and they feasted. After the feast, Swan knelt before Elk and shared all his wisdom. When Swan was done, Elk knelt before Swan and shared all his thoughts and advice.

This is how they learned from one another and were able to look after each other.

This story of Swan, Elk, and their peoples speaks directly to something that I think a lot of us feel: the pressure to be like everyone else, to follow paths that aren't ours because we think they'll bring us security, respect, or a sense of belonging. It's a pattern woven into human nature, especially in times when we feel lost or unsure. In Swan and Elk's story, both sides tried to survive by becoming something they weren't, by trying to act and live like the other. And in that effort they lost sight of their own gifts, their strengths, and ultimately their purpose.

This isn't just a story about animals. It reflects a human truth, a wider condition that shows up everywhere, whether it's individuals, communities, or nations. We see people, companies, and whole systems copying what they think works for others. We mimic each other out of fear and insecurity, out of not wanting to risk failure by doing things differently. But in doing so we end up diluting what's unique about us, the very things that could lead to true balance and harmony.

In today's world there's an endless pressure to compare, to imitate, to match what others are doing so we don't feel left behind. Whether it's in the expectations set by social media, the structures that corporate or government models push us toward, or how we think our communities should look, this pressure to conform is real. Colonial systems have pushed this even further, making us believe that the only way to be successful is to follow Western and colonial ways, to abandon our own teachings in favour of something that looks like progress from the outside.

Swan and Elk's story is a reminder to step back from that need to copy, to trust that our own ways hold the wisdom we need. It shows us that real strength doesn't come from blending in or trying to be what we're not. Swan and Elk didn't succeed by forcing their people to act the same. Instead, they came together to share what each side knew best. They knelt before one another and shared their wisdom openly. That humility, that willingness to acknowledge that the other had something they didn't, created true balance. It wasn't about being right, it was about seeing the bigger picture and honouring each other's gifts.

When I read this story I think about the teachings our elders have shared, and how true strength isn't in uniformity but in diversity. We're strong not because we're all the same but because each of us has something unique to contribute. And I think of how colonial systems have tried to strip us of this by making us feel that our ways aren't enough. But stories like Swan and Elk's remind us that when we try to live by someone else's truth, we weaken ourselves and lose sight of who we are.

As you reflect on this story, think about where in your life you may be following a path that isn't truly yours. Are there parts of you, of your community, that you're holding back or trying to fit into someone else's model? And how might you begin to honour your own gifts, your own way forward, even if it looks different from what others expect? Maybe the freedom we're looking for comes not from keeping up with others but from having the courage to reconnect with who we've always been.

Chapter 15

THE ULTIMATE COYOTE TEACHING

Throughout our territories of the syilx and secwepemc Nations, which extend from parts of the so-called United States of America and into the province of British Columbia, Canada, we have land indicators we call "Coyote markers" that share important stories and teachings.

There is a marker outside of a little town called Falkland, BC. Every time we drove by my mom would point it out and say, "That's Coyote's canoe." I vaguely remember her talking about this canoe, and the only part I remember was the end where he got lazy and just left it there, and continued on.

There is a marker outside of a little place called Soap Lake in Washington State that was shared with me by my friend Willow Abrahamson. We met when we were just kids on the powwow trail and reconnected over the last few years to share teachings and stories.

When I was little my mom would pick up my tema and we would drive all over our territory. My mom and tema would tell stories and point at the lake, or a rock formation in a mountain and share a story about it with me and Evelyn. They were always sharing stories freely with us, just like most of our teachers.

However, there was one story that no one would ever tell me when I would ask about it. We have a significant Coyote marker close to our home, and the image of it is powerful. Some people call it a balancing rock. I grew up knowing this rock had something to do with the world coming to an end as we knew it: if the rock were to fall, it would be a sign that the world was ending or changing.

Every time I would ask people to tell me the story they said I wasn't ready to hear it. Or they told me to ask a certain person, and when I would ask them they would tell me that they couldn't tell me the story unless we were at the place. Other people would tell me I was too young to understand the story. I looked for this story and asked about it for many years, and still it was never shared with me. I thought, *The story will come to me when I am ready.*

In the summer of 2019 I travelled across British Columbia to host circles in communities to talk about violence against women and girls. We wanted to find solutions and build an action plan to support the families of missing and murdered Indigenous women and girls (the original hashtag, #MMIWG, is now #MMIWG2SLGBTQQIA+, for missing and murdered Indigenous women and girls, 2spirit, lesbian, gay, bi-sexual, trans, queer, questioning, intersex, and asexual).

I prepared for this work. I talked to storytellers and elders and did ceremony. I jumped in the water, I did sweat lodge, and I spent time on the land. During this time I would go home and be drawn to Coyote Rock to get strength and grounding. I still didn't know the full story, but I felt a sense of responsibility to be at that place as I did this work.

One of my teachers told me that, as I travelled across the province, to think of it as gathering the bits. We cannot breathe life back into our teachings if we don't have all the bits, and she reminded me about Coyote and Fox. In our stories, Fox was Coyote's twin brother, and the Creator gave him the power to bring Coyote back to life. Many times in our stories Coyote would die and his body would be strewn all over the place. Fox would come along, see what had happened, and go about gathering all the bits. Once Fox had them all he would step over them four times to bring Coyote back to life.

My teachers always reminded me that it was not my job to see the whole picture but to gather the bits and bring them all together. I was also told that if we get to what we think is the end and the picture isn't clear, that means we're missing a bit, or a voice or song, and that our work isn't done. This advice has served me well in cases where I've come to what I thought was the end of a project and things still weren't clear. In the past I would have forced a conclusion to the work to meet the needs of the client. Now I encourage my team to let go of the need to have an end product and focus on the journey.

Centring Indigenous knowledge and ceremony as part of this work was a powerful and emotional experience. It was this work that highlighted the need to focus on coming-of-age as a way to heal our communities. As we travelled across BC I listened to stories and read articles written by our people who have worked hard over the decades to centre Indigenous knowledge in all spaces. Then, one night as I was googling syilx stories, I found a thesis written by Dr. Bill Cohen from our nation. In his paper, he shared the story of Coyote Rock:

> Long ago, Coyote's daughter was afraid of the coming changes. Coyote comforted his daughter and told her that she would be safe from the coming changes if she did as he suggested. He lay on his back and told his daughter she should sit on him [on his penis] and she would be safe. She trusted him and did as directed. As soon as her body touched his penis, however, they both immediately turned to stone.

As I finished reading this tears began to stream down my face. They came for a number of reasons. I cried because this story carried so much meaning in the work I was doing related to #MMIWG. Throughout our journey, people shared the importance of the connection between the violence and degradation of the land and how it directly impacts the violence and degradation of our women. I cried because of all the stories I heard from women and girls and the families of those missing and murdered. I cried because the story came to me in that exact moment and my heart felt lighter. I felt an immense amount of trust and faith in our teachings. I heard my mom's voice in my head saying, "You are exactly where you are meant to be, hearing exactly what you're meant to hear, doing exactly what you're meant to be doing at this exact time."

I also understood the depth and importance and prophecy of this story. Dr. Bill Cohen points out the teaching about consequence when those responsible for children abuse their power by seeking gratification for their own desires rather than treating the children, especially girls, with love, care, and respect. He goes on to point out that this is the only story in which Coyote doesn't get brought back to life. His daughter also turned to stone, representing the symbolic death to the fundamental system of Okanagan society.

The way we treat each other is a reflection of how we treat the land. We are not separate from the land, we are a part of it. Our actions over the last few decades have indicated that we do not love the land; in fact, we abuse it. And so we have not loved ourselves either. We have abused ourselves because of the hopelessness, the silence, the shame, the pain.

This story reminds us of a powerful truth: fear can push us into destructive actions, especially when we feel lost, disconnected, or powerless. Coyote Rock serves as a caution, a lesson to hold close, showing us that when fear is met with harm, toward ourselves or others, we create deeper wounds that don't just affect us in the moment, they ripple out, leaving lasting impacts that we can't always undo. Those wounds move beyond our own lives, settling into the lives of those around us and into the very land we stand on.

When things get hard, when fear threatens to consume us, this story teaches us that real courage is not about fighting or lashing out but staying true to ourselves and our teachings, even in the dark moments. This story is a call to remember that each of us has the power to choose differently, to move forward without causing harm, knowing that the hurt we inflict today can leave scars that may never fully heal.

In honouring this teaching we are reminded that our actions have weight and consequence. Can we learn to pause in those moments of fear and uncertainty? Can we hold space for our pain without letting it turn outward? And can we commit to walking through our struggles in a way that nurtures, rather than harms, the future we leave behind?

Coyote Rock tells us that some actions close doors forever, but it also reminds us that every day we're given a choice to walk in a good way, for ourselves, for each other, and for those who come after us. As we face the unknown, can we hold space for each other's fear and pain without letting it turn to harm? How can we lean on our teachings to guide us through, so that our journey together is one of healing, not hurt?

It has become human nature to run away and numb everything that makes us human. When we are scared and fearful it has become easier to run away and dull the human experience with drugs, alcohol, sex, social media, and gambling. When we want to fix things, we focus on everything outside of us and put all our energy into fixing and healing whatever we see as needy—a family member, the community. We focus all our efforts on saving the planet. Colonialism has taught us that the answer is to just keep numbing the pain, forgetting our humanness, and focusing on the things that make us feel small and helpless.

Coming-of-age helps us understand ourselves, our identity, and our purpose. It gives us the confidence and courage we need to keep moving forward, focusing and contributing in the ways that we know. It helps us understand that we do not have to pretend to be any more than we are in this moment, and that the only thing we have control over in the world is ourselves. When we have the courage to heal ourselves and feel every emotion we were meant to feel as human beings, we learn that with the ability to feel pain also comes the ability to feel love.

When we remember what it is like to feel love we become capable of giving love to the Animal People who gave up their lives to give us the best chance at survival on this earth. And we will understand that loving the land is the same as loving ourselves.

Chapter 16

STANDING BY WATER

The colonial systems we live in today make it hard for us to believe in ourselves. The moment we are born we are told we must be a certain way. As we move through life, pieces of who we were born to be are slowly stripped from us by society's conditioning: we are all born to wake up, go to work, come home, go to sleep, and then do it all again the next day.

This then becomes your identity, and you work to build on it to be successful. And to be successful in this colonial space you must let go of who you are, how you feel, and how you think, and you must stay quiet to move ahead. Don't stir the pot, don't be different.

We are raised to think in a linear fashion, and school reinforces this. Math, English, science—the school systems condition us to obey and listen to the rules. We are graded and compared to each other, and it becomes a competition.

Suddenly all we know is fear. Sometimes it's apparent and sometimes it's hidden. We are scared to be wrong, to look stupid, to be embarrassed. We are worried that if we aren't good at something it means we are stupid. If we don't learn from the way someone is teaching u, we have a learning difference, and that is seen as a deficit. Value is placed on those who fit into the well-constructed system.

If you did something wrong at school, you were shamed or punished. These were called "disciplinary actions," and now many people hear the word "discipline" and react strongly. It doesn't feel like a good word or memory. A question had a right or wrong answer, and if you didn't say the right thing you were told, "You are wrong." Even if the teacher tried to soften the blow with "good try," it still meant you were wrong.

My elders never told me "you are wrong" or "you are right." They always wanted me to share what I knew, what my understanding was. I was encouraged to say whatever I thought and it was valued. Never was I corrected and told, "That is not the right way. *This* is the way." I was always encouraged to tackle problems and solutions based on my own thinking, to start from my knowing and then try it to see if it worked. If it didn't work I was encouraged to try it another way.

If I threw a tantrum or acted badly, my tema, mom, and uncles would tell me to go jump in the creek. They said it would "wash the ick off" me. I was told that when I had a hard time or needed to be grounded I needed to jump in the water. Water was there to discipline my body. Later on my mom told me that practice of jumping in cold water helped us through puberty. It helped us to not be stinky and gave us beautiful clear skin.

My tema had a one-person sweat lodge right by the creek where she would pray or cleanse herself—literally. Not just spiritually but physically as well. Sweat lodge is a good way to get all the dead skin off, and we would be told to use our nails to gently remove it before jumping in the water. My tema didn't use soap bars; instead, she always had smooth, round, black rocks that she got from the creek.

I was told that when you jump in ice-cold water, it purifies your blood. Your skin prickles and brings fire to your blood, cleansing it of impurities and getting rid of any bad energy that your body might be holding on to.

Cold water has been found to help with depression because the cold receptors in your brain are ten times more sensitive than heat receptors, so cold water fires the receptors that overwhelm and shock the brain and release endorphins (the feel-good hormone in your brain), which help ease symptoms of depression and anxiety.

Water teachings are an important part of coming-of-age. Our old people would often instruct our young ones to find their spirit helpers by following the water to its head. It was during that journey that people could find their spirit helper.

Even the sound of water is important, because the animals listen for it. It shows them where to go. The sound of water heals our people, and it is as primary to us as everything else in nature.

Whenever I faced a challenge I would be told to go see my elders. I would tell them the challenge I was facing, and they would listen and tell me go to the water to find my answers. Sometimes I would even seek out my friends who were the same age who I knew carried our stories and teachings, and they would bring me to the water and tell me I would find my answers there.

I would become frustrated because I just wanted them to tell me what to do or what choice to make. I felt like they had all the experience and knowledge and answers, and I just wanted them to give them to me. But they always told me, "That's not the way learning works." Our elders always said things like, "I don't know what is in your head," or, "You already know the answer to that."

I was always impatient, thinking, *If I knew the answer I wouldn't be here.* But instead of saying that out loud I would listen and go to the water. I would look at the water and try to see something symbolic. I would listen hard and close my eyes, trying to hear something speaking to me, or I would look for a sign that would be clear enough to tell me what to do. I never saw anything. Later I learned it was because we weren't supposed to be *looking* for something, we were supposed to be listening.

Something magical happens when you stand by water. If you've ever taken this time, whether by a creek, river, lake, or ocean, you know how hypnotizing it can be. This is what our teachers meant when they said the sound is medicine.

When you are struggling or living in trauma and feeling challenged, you are moving into the stem part of your brain that makes it hard to concentrate and find solutions. Trauma can change the chemicals in the brain, as well as its structure. Trauma and stress impact us in more ways than we realize. Many times we think we are okay and brush things off, minimizing what we are going through. We are told to suck it up. When we are challenged and not feeling well, or our brain is living in a place of trauma, we feel unsafe and confused. We can't think clearly, we can't focus, we feel like there is no solution. We feel hopeless.

When we feel safe we move from the lower part of our brain that won't allow us to concentrate into the part that is beautiful and creative, where the solutions lie. We can think clearly. We feel good and can focus. And so, as we stand by the water listening to its healing sounds, the waves, the rushing, we begin to feel safe. We feel calm and content. If we stand or sit by the water long enough and focus on the sound, we move into the part of us that is brilliant.

There's a reason why our best ideas come when we're in the shower—the water brings about our best thinking. The moment our mind and body and spirit began to feel that love and safety, our brain lights up at our spirit coming back to guide us.

We are all related. Each and every one of us spent the first nine months of our lives surrounded by water. We were born from water. Our bodies are made up of 60 percent of it. Our hearts are 75 percent water and our brains are 80 percent. It is only natural to feel connected and safe, like you belong, when you stand by the water.

Every time I looked to my elders and teachers they encouraged me to keep moving forward. They never gave me the answers, they told me I needed to go to the land or the water. They always told me to start everything with ceremony and end in ceremony.

Ceremony doesn't have to be a big deal. It doesn't need a medicine person or healer, and it doesn't need to be a big show. It can be something just for you, whatever feels good. Your instinct knows how to take care of you. Each one of us is a healer and helper.

We cannot heal or help anyone but ourselves, and that work will be felt by everyone around us. It is all we can do. We cannot do this work for anyone else because they must do it themselves, and that is one of the hardest things for us to accept. We have been taught to believe that everyone else has the answer, that others are better or smarter because of their standing, their position, their title or age.

We are told to rely on experts and not trust ourselves, so we wait for permission, for validation. We wait for a pat on the head before we continue to move forward.

Whenever I asked one of my teachers, "Is this the right way?" they would never say yes. They wanted me to learn how to use what they taught me in my own way. I was so confused—*How in the world am I supposed to do it their way when I'm not them?* It makes sense now, as I've grown to trust myself, but for the longest time I was stuck, frozen, not knowing where to go or what to do because I was waiting for something or someone to show me the way. But the thing is, no one can walk my path for me or tell me how to walk it. We must all walk our own paths.

There have been a few times when I've shared teachings connected to focusing on healing and self-love when I've been called out and told, "We must not be selfish or become narcissists—the world makes us think we have to be the centre of everything." When we think of only ourselves we become selfish, self-absorbed. This is another example of how we've been conditioned: we can take concepts about self-love and turn them into fear-based thinking, which makes us selfish.

When we focus on healing ourselves, on being our best selves, we feel good, we love and trust ourselves, and we can step into the world as the best version of us. Then we can be a good person, a good family and community member, and when we are finally all of those things we can respect the land and give back without rules or expectations, or the need to get something back. We don't feel resentment or fear.

Focusing on everyone else can be draining. Our body feels it and we get sick. We become resentful, waiting for someone else to help us or save us. Because we put so much out we expect it back. We do this until we burn out and get sick, depressed, and overwhelmed. We wonder why no one gives back to us like we give to them. We get irritable and snappy and our body feels it. We do not feel good about ourselves, which our family and community feels. Our land feels it too.

The way we feel about ourselves impacts the way we make decisions for our family, our community, and our land. If we contribute to our families and communities from a place of anger or depression or hopelessness, we do not move forward. When we question ourselves and are not confident, we often stay silent because we do not want to be judged. We don't think like others, we don't talk or act like them, so we stay quiet and don't contribute. And even when we do, we don't contribute from our light but from the darkness.

The more we teach ourselves how to be confident, to rely on our own thinking and instincts, the better we are for everything else. When we are confident it doesn't matter what anyone else says because we won't take it personally. What they say and how they act won't hold us back from showing up in our light. We stay bright even when people try to make us dim.

In the old days we didn't focus on the self to be self-absorbed, we did so because we understood that it was required of us to bring our best selves forward so we could contribute to our family, community, and land. We understood that whatever we did as individuals impacted everything around us.

My mom passed away in 2017, twenty-one years after the stroke that left her unable to speak. After her funeral our family was told to go to the creek and use the water to wash our arms and legs and heads so that we could leave the grief there, and to help get rid of the grief of others that we might be holding on to. Others' grief isn't for us to hold.

I use water for protection and grounding, especially when I'm nervous or upset. When I host circles where I know there are going to be big emotions I will grab a glass of water, one that I don't drink from, and put it in the middle of the circle. It helps hold the energy in the room. When we are done I pour the water out by a tree or a rock. If I am travelling on my own and staying in a hotel where we cannot burn medicine, I use water to help me. I will pour some into a glass, put my finger into it, say a prayer, and let the water take away everything I'm holding on to. Sometimes I cry, sometimes I don't—I trust my body to do what it needs to.

All these teachings were given so that I would know how to take care of myself and make sure that I was doing things to nurture my spirit. They were little things that I was raised with, and I was never given a reason for them. It was simply the way it was done.

When I was being raised by my tema, I remember feeling confident. I felt like I walked around just knowing things. My family called me *élćalpt*, which meant "to be fierce" or "awesome," because my tema said I was so smart I was scary. Also because I knew how to take care of myself and never seemed afraid.

When I was little and spent time with my mom when she was drinking, I knew how to take care of myself, and Evelyn. My family would let me leave the house to go wander and play outside when I was as young as four.

I would take Evelyn, two years younger than me, and we would wander into the hills, playing out there and climbing the clay banks. We would even wander off the reserve and into town when I was a toddler, finding ways to get about. When I looked at my four-year-old son I couldn't imagine him wandering out and about with a two-year-old in tow.

I felt like nothing scared me when I was a little girl but I did feel an immense sense of responsibility over Evelyn, to take care of her and make sure she was fed and clothed. I knew even at that age I was even responsible for keeping her alive. This fearlessness was a part of who I was out on the rez. I had a deep sense of faith that we were being taken care of and watched over by something we couldn't see.

Things began to change as I got older and was introduced to the outside world. I started school and extracurricular activities off the reserve. From birth to the age of five I had spent all my time on the Penticton Indian Band reserve with my tema. I rarely went into town. When I did it was with my tema, and I had to help her get up and walk. I had to learn to stand as strong and stiff as I could to help her—she used a cane most of the time but preferred to use me as her support.

My tema was slow in everything she did but I didn't mind. I always felt so proud of her. In our community our elders were always treated special. They got the best and comfiest seats at ceremony and events, and our people and leaders went out of their way to make sure they were comfortable and fed first.

They always got to go to the front of the line, and I always happily escorted my tema wherever she needed to go. She also needed a translator out in the world—she would say things in our language and I would tell the lady at the bank or the cashier at the store what she needed. My tema couldn't read or write English and she signed her checks at the bank with a little wobbly x, which I thought was cool.

My uncles tell me a story about a time I was six and walked with my tema into the bank to find a long line. I took her by the hand and started walking by everyone in line, saying, "Excuse me, my tema is coming through. She's an elder," and my tema was surprised to see everyone smile down at me and move aside for her. I didn't think twice about it. I did it because that's the way I was raised. I didn't realize that not everyone had the same regard for elders outside of our community.

I was confident in everything I did—until I started elementary school. Once I started kindergarten I slowly began to doubt myself. My first day of school is imprinted in my mind forever. I remember being so happy to be at school that I ran as fast as I could to the door, and on the way another little girl tripped me. When I fell to the ground I hit my face on the cement and got a bloody nose. The little girl called me a "wagon burner."

From that day on, every time I was at school I heard things like "wagon burner, squaw, dirty Indian," and I knew I was different and not seen as good enough. My first anxiety attack happened when I was five and they continued from there. I would spend many days outside my classroom breathing into a paper bag, trying to get air into my lungs. My heart and spirit hurt so badly I couldn't breathe.

I didn't understand that my anxiety and inability to breathe was linked to my inability to cry. There were lots of multigenerational reasons why I didn't, but mostly because my uncles told me to never cry because it was a long way from my heart. They would say that physical pain should be toughed out.

When I started to get bullied my uncles told me I needed to learn how to fight. They said I had to be just as smart back, and that I had to be fast because if I ever punched someone, I either had to be tougher or faster. But above all else, they told me, "Never, ever let them see you cry." So I didn't. Instead, I had anxicty and panic attacks.

My uncles told me we weren't allowed to cry because that's what their dads had told them, that it showed weakness. Other people in my family said that "never let them see you cry" meant "don't let the white people see you cry." Don't let them know they hurt you. It was something children were told in residential school. If they saw you cry you would be a target.

I had a different way of seeing and sharing things, and people didn't understand what I was trying to say. When I would talk about the Animal People, or Coyote or Owl Woman, kids would look at me like I was crazy.

When I saw kids acting up or doing bad things, I would point it out to them and tell them they shouldn't do it because of a Coyote teaching I had heard. They would ask me why, or how, or where I had heard it from. Then they would tell the teacher I was telling lies or trying to scare them and I would get in trouble for making things up.

I learned I had to be careful with what I said because sometimes I would talk about spirits bugging us, or Little People playing tricks on us, or hearing ancestors talk to me. I learned that hearing and seeing and believing in these things meant something was wrong with you.

It also meant a trip to the school counsellor, who would ask me if I was seeing things, or they would say, "Do you see them now?" Whenever a teacher would pull me aside to talk to me or ask me questions, I didn't understand what was going on but I could feel that I was doing something bad, so I began to question everything I knew.

I was told that my way of thinking was superstitious and outdated, and as I became a teenager I was informed that some of the experiences I was having were warning signs of a mental health issue, that the things I experienced were hallucinations, or my mind was playing tricks on me. I learned to be quiet because I didn't want people to think I was crazy.

I started to lose trust and faith and confidence in myself. I didn't know the basic terms that they knew about living in their society, so I started to learn silence. I learned to keep quiet about what I thought because it didn't make sense to them. They laughed at me when I told them about the creek by our house and the living beings in it, and how we should have respect for the fish when you killed them so they didn't suffer.

They thought I was crazy or lying when I told them about the Little People and the Water People, and as I got older I began to question my spirituality and wonder if it was folklore or things I had made up in my head as a child.

By the time I got to high school I was angry. By then I had spent the first ten years of my life with an alcoholic mother, and I felt abandoned and unloved. I had spent every day of my childhood hearing how stupid and ugly I was, how I didn't belong.

As I moved through high school and became a young adult, I wanted to be taken seriously. I wanted to do good in school and maybe get a degree, but because I had a hard time with math I couldn't get into a post-secondary school in Canada, and I resigned myself to believing I was stupid and that I would never make it. These things drove the way I made decisions for myself. I was losing my sense of identity, and I began to question my teachings and ways of knowing. I ran away from it all.

When you hear these things every day of your life you begin to believe them, so by the age of twelve I had started to drink heavily. I became violent and spiteful. I talked back to anyone who made me feel small. I ignored all the things I was taught as a little girl, even though I felt awful for not following certain protocols. In my gut I felt like I was doing something wrong by not listening to what was taught to me.

Drinking helped me forget the bad stuff. It helped me forget the pain. It hardened me up and I liked the feeling of not caring, of being numb and unemotional. When you drink as much as I did you lose every part of yourself that makes you unique. The spirit in the bottle replaced my own, and I spent many years without my spirit. I lied, stole, cheated, and manipulated and hurt people. I experienced so many dark days, and I felt lonely and left behind.

There were moments in my life that could have changed who I was forever, opportunities that presented themselves to me that could have killed me or put me in jail. In those moments I felt something. I heard my tema's voice and I felt her hands on my back. I did a lot of bad things in my life, but I could have done worse. It was my tema's spirit and her spirit helper that kept me alive.

It took me over a decade to work through the many traumas I'd experienced to find myself again. I began to work towards sobriety from alcohol because it numbed me. It covered over my memories of abuse and shame. I drank to hide. I drank to run away.

It took me a decade to finally stay away from alcohol completely, because every time I would stay dry I would remember things, feelings of hurt and pain and confusion. I didn't know how to handle it all so I would start to drink again. I drank to forget everything.

Even after I started on my healing journey and stayed sober so I could think clearly, it took me a little while to start using my real voice again. It took me a long time to share the things I knew out loud. I still feared backlash and people telling me I was wrong. I feared people insinuating that I didn't know what I was talking about, so I continued to play small and dumb.

I got involved with business and politics and started getting invited to meetings with millionaires and leaders. I was a good Indian girl who didn't question the way things were done or what was said. I knew my place if I wanted to be successful and make it in that world. I was an "Indigenous consultant," but I was really a consultant who happened to be Indigenous.

Then, just as I thought I was "getting ahead," something happened that forced me to deal with my trauma. Someone groped me inappropriately, and the next thing I knew I was in full-blown PTSD mode, but what it looked like to others was a midlife crisis. I learned all about the patriarchy and its power during that experience, and it changed my life forever. I could no longer pretend that the world of business and politics I was participating in was okay.

It was time to heal, to deal with the feelings I was running away from, or I was going to start drinking again and I would die from it. What got me through was ceremony, songs, and the medicine of our people. It was in that moment that I decided I could no longer pretend I was small and stay quiet. I could no longer uphold systems of harm and pretend it was okay.

When I started sharing the teachings of my tema and mom again, people thought I was naive and didn't think that my teachings were going to be useful in business or politics or community. For the first while I believed them and held back. But as I continued to push the limits, I learned that our teachings really are magic. It was a magic that I couldn't explain or validate to people in the terms they wanted me to, but they knew that what I was doing was worth trying out because what they were doing wasn't working.

I have also found that the longer I stay sober, the more teachings I remember. Drinking helped me forget the pain and the bad memories, but it also meant that I forgot the love and the good memories and stories.

Colonialism taught me that I was too much and too weird. It taught me that I was ugly and talked too much. It taught me that I did everything backwards and took the long way round. It taught me that I wasn't worthy for certain spaces because I didn't have a degree or education. It made me doubt everything I was and made me believe that to be successful I had to give up my humanness to fit in, so I dimmed my light.

Coming-of-age taught me who I am, where I come from, and what my purpose is. I have strong senses of identity, connection, and belonging, and I was raised to watch how I walk in this world because I not only represent myself but my family, my community, and my nation. It has taught me that in this life I will experience heartache and pain, but I have everything I will ever need to know to go through it. And every time I do, I become stronger.

Coming-of-age reminds me to share the stories of where I come from, the "people of the stories," the "people with the power to dream," and we have a responsibility to collect and weave understandings of the world and intertwine ourselves within the tmix^w and its regenerative capacity. I know who I am, where I come from, and what I am here to do.

We are born as humans, and as humans we will feel pain. There will be days when we will struggle to find a way. On those days, remember to go to the water.

Stand by the water. And as you do so, close your eyes and listen to it. Allow that feeling of peace, serenity, connection, and love to wash over you. Feel connected. Feel your belonging. Feel safe.

And as you feel these things you will feel yourself moving into the best part of your mind, body, and spirit, and you will think clearly. You will be motivated. You will be able to uncover solutions. You will find the answers and you will no longer struggle.

On the day I was born my tema welcomed me into the world by telling me, "Your name is teɬxnitk^w." She wouldn't tell me what my name really meant; she said I would find out later. "You'll know when you're supposed to know."

I finally learned that my name translates to "Standing by Water."

What was it that our elders were teaching us when they sent us to the water? Self-determination. They were teaching us that despite what the world today has taught us to believe, we are born with everything we will ever need to know.

Chapter 17

COMING HOME

When I started writing this book in 2020, I knew there was more I wanted to say, more than I had told in *Calling My Spirit Back*. That book was about finding my voice, but this one felt different. I wanted this book to be more than my story. I wanted it to be something that could help others on their own path, something that could support healing in a real, meaningful way.

The first draft of this book came together at the end of 2021, but I knew then it wasn't finished. I thought I had made it to the other side of my own coming-of-age work, only to discover that there was still so much waiting for me. There were lessons I hadn't fully learned, boundaries I hadn't set, and truths I hadn't yet faced. And 2023 became the year those lessons hit me square in the face.

In early 2023 I made the choice to leave Alderhill Planning Inc., the company I had founded and poured so much of myself into. Leaving wasn't easy. It was one of the hardest decisions of my life, but it was necessary. I stayed there and made excuses that I was there for everyone else. I told myself I was the one the employees could depend on to support their well-being, even when the weight was pulling me down. I cared deeply for the people I brought into the company. I wanted to shield them from the instability and stress and high expectations that came with the work. I thought that, if I just held on tighter, things would get better.

But the truth was, Alderhill was costing me more than I could continue to give. I was sacrificing my own well-being, my own spirit, to stay in a place that no longer aligned with who I was becoming. Leaving Alderhill was my first real act of self-respect in a long time. I had to walk away without the closure I had hoped for, knowing that this part of my story might never feel fully resolved. That was the lesson: to learn to move forward without needing everything resolved, without having my heart at peace.

After leaving Alderhill I focused on my new company, Naqsmist Storytellers Inc., pouring my energy into building something that felt aligned with my values and purpose. But that journey brought its own set of challenges. As the year went on it became clear that the financial reality of Naqsmist meant I had to make a decision that felt like a punch to the gut: I had to let go of 70 percent of my employees. I held on to them far longer than I should have because I wanted to be loved and accepted as their leader, and I wanted to take care of them. I felt responsible for them. I thought if I just worked harder, took on more of the burden, I could carry us all through.

But the truth is, real leadership sometimes means making the hard calls, the ones that don't make you popular, the ones that people might not understand. I wanted to keep everyone afloat, to be the kind of leader who could save us all. But holding on that way became a lesson in letting go.

And just when I thought I couldn't take any more lessons, life handed me another one, but this time it was personal. The summer of 2024 brought a challenge that demanded my full attention. My daughter was going through one of the most difficult times of her life, and she reached out for help in a way that left no room for anything else. So I stopped everything. I put the business on hold. I stopped trying to carry everyone else and poured myself into being there for her, for our family. It was a reminder, a painful one, that none of this is worth anything if I can't be there for my own children.

In August of that year we moved back to my community, the Penticton Indian Band. Living away had shown me who I was beyond the roles and expectations that come with being part of a tight-knit community. It taught me to set boundaries, to learn who I am without everyone else's voices shaping me. But coming back now, after years of healing, felt different. It was an invitation to be my full self, to bring everything I had learned about love, boundaries, and truth back to the place where it all started.

Returning to my community meant facing old patterns—people-pleasing, fear of judgment, the need for approval—but this time I felt ready. I had done the work and unpacked the survival tactics that had kept me small, quiet, and compliant. Growing up here I learned early how to walk that line between speaking up and staying silent. I was always afraid of causing waves, of being shunned for the connections I chose, for the relationships I valued. But now I'm here with a commitment to show up as who I am—not to appease, not to fit in, but to be true to myself.

I came back home knowing it would be a stretch, that it would ask things of me I hadn't anticipated. But I'm here, willing to try. I'm here to walk alongside my people, to share what I've learned, to bring the love I've cultivated back into this place. Coming-of-age, for me, has been about learning to let go of that need for approval, to stop shrinking in the face of others' discomfort. This book, this journey, has given me a chance to confront the old survival tactics that still creep in and tell me to hold back, to soften my words, to not be too much.

Each of these steps—writing *Coming of Age,* leaving Alderhill, facing difficult decisions with Naqsmist, standing by my daughter, and, finally, coming home—each has been a part of this journey. Each one has taught me that coming-of-age isn't a single moment, it's a process, an unfolding, a peeling back of layers, and a willingness to stand in my own truth.

When I began writing this book in 2020 my purpose was to show that real change doesn't come from fighting for power within the systems we currently rely on, like chief, council, or other elected roles. These structures we fight over aren't where our true strength lies. If we truly want self-determination, if we're serious about shifting our paths, we have to start with the work we do within ourselves. We need to face our trauma and overcome it so we can show up grounded, regulated, and courageous. That's where our power is. True self-determination doesn't come from seizing roles in these systems, it's about building the strength to live by a way that's truly ours.

Self-determination isn't handed to us through government meetings or signed papers. It grows from the work we do within ourselves—from healing, from reclaiming our power, and from coming of age in a way that reconnects us to our strength and purpose. It's about developing the courage to lead differently, to live by our own teachings, and to honour the power that's already within us. When we do this we don't just fill roles created by others, we redefine what leadership and change mean in our own terms, guided by a vision that is truly ours.

This final chapter has become a reflection on the many stages of coming-of-age that have defined my life. Each has brought me closer to understanding what it truly means to walk my talk, to stand in my truth, and to embody the teachings I hope to pass down to my daughter: to be true to herself, even when it's uncomfortable, even when it causes friction. Writing this book has pushed me beyond my comfort zone. I always thought of myself as honest and open, but there were things I was still holding back.

Funny enough, as I started writing and reached the acknowledgments, I found myself face to face with my own struggle, my own coming-of-age. I wanted to honour the people whose impact on my life has been profound, even if that meant stirring up memories that might feel complicated or bittersweet to others. When I wrote *Calling My Spirit Back*, I held back. I tiptoed around fully acknowledging people, afraid of causing hurt or leaving someone out. I wanted people to like me, to accept my words without feeling challenged. I didn't want my words to make someone feel like my experiences with people diminished their experiences. I never saw myself as someone who held back, but these last few years have shown me how deeply I've internalized that need for acceptance and approval.

This realization has been part of my coming-of-age, a lesson in stepping forward without apologizing for how I experience people and the world. Some might think I'm naive, but they don't know the years I spent in darkness, cynicism, and pain, navigating the shadows of politics and business. I became pretty good at it, seeing firsthand how people could manipulate and be manipulated. I know that as human beings, we are both good *and* bad, right *and* wrong.

When I began to move away from that world of politics and business, and when I started leaning back into the teachings my tema gave me, my heart shifted. I learned to hold both the pain and hope together, to carry the weight of our stories and still find room for light.

This process of writing and acknowledging the people who have shaped me has been a way of making peace with my journey and all those who travelled alongside me. It's a step into my truth, a recognition that I'm no longer afraid to see things as they are, to speak openly of what I've learned, and to honour the complexities in my path. I hope that by embracing my full experience I'm teaching my daughter, and anyone reading, that there is strength in standing fully in who we are, in honouring all the hands that have helped shape us, even when it's complicated, even when it brings up a mix of emotions.

This is what it means to come of age. It's not about becoming a perfect version of ourselves, it's about continually peeling back layers, releasing what no longer serves us, and standing taller in our story with each passing day. It's taken me a long time to feel free to acknowledge others openly, to celebrate the beauty of those who have impacted me, without worrying about how others might interpret it.

I recognize there's still hurt here, wounds that go back generations, and these divide us in ways that tear at my heart. And yet I still hold on to hope. Hope that we can heal, that we can learn to come together, even with all our complexities.

Each stage of my journey has shown me that coming-of-age is not a single moment, it's a process of shedding what no longer serves us and stepping into deeper layers of ourselves. It's about knowing that being true to ourselves will sometimes cause discomfort and learning to accept that. Walking our talk means being willing to carry both the light and shadow of our truths, to make space for healing within ourselves and our communities.

I am learning bit by bit to let go of the need to be liked, to stop shrinking in the face of others' discomfort, and to offer my truth without apology. This book has given me a chance to practice that, to confront the old survival tactics urging me to soften my words or hold back. But I know now that telling my story means telling it fully. It takes courage, a willingness to stand in the light and shadow of my experiences.

As I look back, I see how each stage of coming-of-age has prepared me for this moment, sharing my story and honouring the people and places that have shaped me, even when it's complicated.

As I close this book, I honour this process, not just for myself but for my daughter, and for all of us who are still on this path. I hope my story serves as a reminder that we can find our way back to ourselves, that we can heal and grow, and that every part of our journey, no matter how complex, is worth honouring. In doing so I hope we create a foundation for healing, resilience, and hope, one that connects us all in our shared humanity.

ACKNOWLEDGEMENTS

Nothing of me is original. I carry the stories, teachings and strength of my ancestors, my community, and every person who has shaped me. I am the collective effort of everyone who has walked with me, guided me and inspired me.

A memory that stands out to me is from when I was twelve years old at a community meeting in the PIB Hall. The province of British Columbia had come to negotiate with us about taking down a blockade that was preventing workers from going to Apex ski resort to work on a development that was threatening our watershed.

Our spokespeople were Grand Chief Stewart Phillip, Dr. Jeannette Armstrong, Greg Gabriel, and Pierre Kruger, and each brought their own strength into that room. They were individuals with unique voices and perspectives yet they moved as one, united in purpose and unwavering in their commitment to our people. Watching them was like seeing resilience and dignity woven together, a living example of what it means to stand in your power without letting anyone shake it.

For an Indian girl from the rez, watching our leaders hold their ground against the province was one of the proudest moments of my life. I could feel the authority and confidence radiating from them as they tag-teamed the provincial representatives who were so clearly trying to hold on to their power and assert control over us. But our leaders didn't flinch. They didn't buckle under pressure or lose their sense of who they were. Instead they showed me what real strength looks like, power that comes from being rooted in purpose, in knowing exactly who you are and who you represent.

That moment became foundational in my understanding of respect and leadership. It showed me that true leadership is not about fitting into systems or appeasing those in authority, it's about holding on to your truth, even when the whole room tries to shift you away from it. They didn't compromise their values or their people's dignity to make things easier. They pushed back with grace and power and showed me what it looks like to lead without apology. They became my heroes.

To my Uncle Steve Basil—Nir'kus'chin, the bridge, the protector, the teacher.

The hours we spent visiting, those evenings on the couch with you and Aunty Janice, gave me strength in ways I didn't even realize at the time. Sitting there, listening, sharing stories, I learned to trust in myself—to know that what I have experienced, what I see, what I feel, is the truth. You helped me see that my way of moving through this world is not just valid, but necessary.

You moved through this world with purpose, with wisdom, with a love so deep that it wove itself into the lives of those around you. You taught us not just with words, but with the way you carried yourself—with patience, with intention, with the understanding that every detail matters. You didn't just walk the land; you knew it, felt it, belonged to it. And you made sure we did too.

You reminded us that our ways are not just things we believe in, but things we live. That every preparation, every ceremony, every small act of care carries meaning. That to hold onto our ways, we must be willing to do the work—to pay attention, to listen, to walk the long road, one step at a time, no shortcuts.

You fought for our people, our lands, our voices, and our future. You made space for those who had none, stood beside those who needed strength, and passed on teachings that will carry far beyond your time here.

I carry you with me. We all do. In the work we continue, in the voices we hold steady, in the love we pass forward.

Lím ləmt, Uncle. You gave us more than we can ever measure.

My godfather and hereditary chief, Adam Eneas, has been more than just a relative, he has been an uncle, a sponsor, a mentor, and a father figure, providing me with unwavering support and guidance. His wife, Sandi Detjen, has been a wonderful momma to me, her presence gentle yet deeply inspiring. Together they have played a crucial role in my healing journey, supporting my sobriety and encouraging me to step into my power as a confident businesswoman. Their influence has been a steady reminder that I am capable, that I have what it takes to walk this path with strength, grace, and purpose.

This book is for my elders, teachers, and relatives who have shared their stories, words, and wisdom so generously, who have surrounded me with love, safety, and a sense of belonging, many who are no longer on this earth anymore but who remain inspirations to our community and nation: my tema, Ellen Alec; my "other tema," Angeline Eneas; Louise Gabriel; Annie Kruger; Agnes and Abe Paul; Rachel and Basil Paul; Vera Gabriel; Dorothy Ward.

To Muggy Baptiste, Chickie Gabriel, Larry Kenoras, Eliza Terbasket, Susan Ortland-George, Richard Armstrong, Dr. Bill Cohen, Lauren Terbasket, Emory Gabriel, and Smuxaken Pierre, each of you has contributed to the roots that keep me grounded, and your teachings have become a part of me that I carry forward. Thank you for guiding me and for making me feel important, seen, and valued in this journey.

To Ethel Kruger, who was always there for my mom, my sister, and me. Thank you for being our aunty, our lookout, and the steady hand that kept us in line. You were a constant presence and a guiding force, and we are forever grateful for the love and care you gave us.

Ryan Day, my lifelong partner and husband, my teacher and friend. You have helped me unlearn the protective behaviours I developed as a child and relearn to live from a place of love and pride for who I am. Your encouragement to question and challenge has been essential, and your conversations continue to guide me in the work I do and the words I write. Nothing I create today truly belongs to me alone, it's a combination of everything we are together, woven with your love, wisdom, and unwavering belief in me. Thank you for being my anchor and my mirror on this journey.

Above all, I want to honour my children for choosing me to be their mom, even with all my imperfections.

My oldest son, Kyle, the son of the late Davis George and me, has been my greatest teacher and guardian angel. He has shown me what forgiveness and true love really mean.

My daughter, Phoenix, whose name was inspired by the Phoenix Process, came to me at a time when I decided to believe in myself. She has been my greatest teacher in self-regulation, showing me what true courage is.

My youngest, Teslin, has taught me to slow down, to huggle, to smile, and to take a moment to love and be present. He reminds me to let go and truly live.

To my nephew, Foxxy, who has been like a son to me, you show me what it means to be both gentle and fierce. You are a fighter and a leader, and you've taught me how big love can be, even when it's not born from your own body.

My adopted daughter, Raven, embodies love, service, and giving. You challenge me to slow down, to find ways to connect, and to feel worthy of being in my kids' spaces, even when I sometimes feel like I'm in the way.

And to my daughter-in-law, Sierra, one of our family's matriarchs who has brought boundless love, gentleness, and heart into our lives, you have been a light in our family during our darkest times. Thank you for shining.

To my sisters, Wynette, Evelyn, and Emma-Lena, my rocks, my laughter, my support in every way. For your unwavering faith, the countless hours you've poured into building a company that has helped support our entire family at one time or another, your dedication means everything to me. You've believed in this journey even when I've doubted, and you've stood beside me, working long hours to help lift this vision higher. You've shown up since day one with so much love, laughter, and strength. I wouldn't be able to do what I do without you—your dedication, your free labour, all the babysitting, the endless meals to keep me alive, and the way you make everything feel possible. You remind me of my worth, make me laugh until I can't breathe, and believe in me so fiercely that I can't help but believe in myself too. Together you three have built me up in ways I can't fully express. You make me feel like the funniest, smartest, and most capable person in the world, and I am so grateful for your love. Thank you for being my sisters, my strength, my family. I carry you with me in everything I do.

To my soul sister, Laurie Buffalo, you are a true gift from the Creator. You show up like no one else can, and you always seem to know exactly when I need you most. Thank you for the prayers, the ceremonies, and for lifting me—sometimes literally—and carrying me through the fire when I can barely stand. You've built me up, even when I felt burned and ready to let go. You've shown me strength, resilience, and unwavering love, and there is no one in this world like you. Period.

My dear friend, business partner, and mentor, Chief Christopher Derrickson, has been someone in my life who has seen the best parts of me when I tried to shrink, and encouraged me to step into the leader I didn't know I was.

To my co-parent and best friend, Paul Rob "Kasp" Sawan, thank you for always showing up, for being there without a second thought. There's so much I could say about you and our journey together, but above all I am grateful for the way you navigate life and for how you show up in the world, even if it drives me bonkers sometimes. I see the strength and love you bring to our kids and to those around you, and I know that our lives are richer because of it. Thank you for being exactly who you are.

To my cousin, Rosalie Yazzie, for the long calls, the mentoring, the love, the dessert dates, the tears and laughter, for your fierceness and your gentleness and for your help through some of my most vulnerable moments.

To my friend, writer, and editor, Delaine Zwiek, you have no idea how your presence and backing has given me the confidence to step into spaces I wasn't sure I could keep up with.

To my brother, Nacoma George, and Crystal Adolph for all of the love, the friendship, the laughter, and the heartfelt connection.

To Suzanne Johnson and Reg Ogen and Talon Ogen. Thank you for the love you have for our family but most of all, thank you for the safety, belonging and connection you've cultivated for Phoenix. I hope you know how much your love has helped us through some of our hardest and darkest times. No words can express my gratitude for your friendship.

To Karen Gabriel and Jon Felker, who taught me about growing up, responsibility, and boundaries. You both took care of me and loved me during some of my darkest times. Your support helped me find stability and strength.

To Anona Kampe, my friend, my colleague, my cousin, my sister, reconnecting to you in our adult years and working with you on our comprehensive community plan has brought some of the most beautiful memories, laughter, tears, and healing into my life.

To my beautiful friends, Joey and Nicole, thank you for the purest kind of friendship, where there's nothing needed but my company. You make me feel cool, truly seen, and loved for exactly who I am. You two are the definition of ride-or-dies, and friendships like this are rare. No toxic history, no heavy expectations, just an easy, joyful connection that reminds me of what friendship should feel like.

To my kin from the Penticton Indian Band, my kin within the syilx nation, thank you. You have shaped me, challenged me, and taught me resilience. You made me a warrior.

To the chiefs and leaders I've supported, learned from, and worked alongside, in particular Chief Jonathan Kruger and Chief Chad Eneas, Regional Chief Shane Gottfriedson, this journey hasn't been easy. I know the challenges you all have faced, the internal battles, the hurts, and the impact these experiences have left on your lives and the lives of your families. Your strength in navigating these hardships is deeply honoured here. I see you and I love you and I know the beautiful leaders and men that you are.

To my team and supporters, past and present, at Naqsmist, you are some of the most brilliant and innovative people I've ever known. I'm constantly in awe of your minds, your passion, and your ability to bring ideas to life. Kyle, Sierra, Laurie, Wynette, Michelyn, Jade, Shane, Anna, Jake, Ylan, Lydia, Moe, Khamil, Gretchen, Bree, BeeVee Professional, and Jen Green, thank you for taking a chance on me. Your faith in this vision and the ways you have each contributed has inspired me.

To all our 2022 and 2023 Certified Cultivating Safe Spaces Facilitators, you have no idea how much impact each of our interactions have had on me.

A special thank you to Jeff and Robyn Ward and your team at Animikii for your belief and support in Cultivating Safe Spaces, and most of all in me, for all of your love and good energy, your coaching, your cheerleading, your pure goodness. Words won't ever be enough to capture the purity and realness of your friendship and support.

To the writers who inspire me and have been there to cheer me on and encourage me: Asha Frost, Kaitlin Curtice, Jen Pastiloff, Helen Knott, Anne Bérubé, Lori Simeunovic, and Lee Spence. You are all powerful forces, and your love and encouragement have given me the strength to feel like I belong in this space. Thank you for seeing me. Thank you for showing me the way, for reminding me that my voice matters, and for making this journey feel like home.

To my business coach, Nick Matheson, thank you for helping me believe in myself as a boss, a leader, a CEO and not letting up even when I tuned out.

To my editor at Tellwell, Simon Ogden, whose very first piece of feedback gave me the courage to dive fully into my first book. Thank you for supporting me to become the writer I wanted to be, for guiding me to trust my own voice, and for your belief in the stories I carry. Your encouragement meant more than words can express, and I'm grateful for the journey we took together.

I would also like to acknowledge my counsellor, who meets with me every other Thursday at 4:00 p.m. Our conversations have helped me overcome things I never thought I'd be able to release. She's challenged me to look closely at the deep-seated beliefs I was raised on, questioning the teachings I've held tightly and asking me, "Do you think your ancestors shared these lessons with the intent for you to feel guilt and shame?" Together we unpacked what it means to be productive, to mother, to be patient, and to love myself deeply. We explored what it truly means to be humble amid growing success.

Through this work I've found confidence in myself, piece by piece. Committing time to my healing and pushing myself to let go of things I no longer needed to hold on to has been uncomfortable yet necessary. To be self-determining, to fully trust myself and my knowledge, I had to do this hard work. Without this foundation I wouldn't have been able to write this book.

ABOUT THE AUTHOR

Elaine Alec, known in nsyilxcen as teɬkənitkʷ (Standing By Water), is a visionary author, entrepreneur, and advocate for Indigenous knowledge and equity. A proud member of the syilx (Okanagan) and secwepemc (Shuswap) nations, Elaine draws from her cultural roots and ancestral teachings to foster transformative spaces of belonging, healing, and empowerment.

As the founder of Naqsmist Storytellers Inc. and creator of the Indigenous-led Cultivating Safe Spaces framework, Elaine has trained over 200 facilitators and impacted thousands globally. By blending traditional Indigenous teachings with contemporary leadership practices, she champions emotional safety and resilience across diverse communities. Her acclaimed memoir, *Calling My Spirit Back*, and her work in decolonized leadership have earned her widespread recognition, including being named one of BCBusiness Magazine's Women of the Year for Equity and Inclusion.

In *Coming of Age*, teɬkənitkʷ shares her journey of healing and resilience while inviting readers to reconnect with their identity, reclaim their humanness, and embrace the lifelong path of self-determination and growth.

Manufactured by Amazon.ca
Acheson, AB

30611376R00118